Connect *with* English

Instructor's Manual to accompany

CONVERSATION BOOKS 1–4

prepared by JANET BATTISTE

Boston, Massachusetts   Burr Ridge, Illinois   Dubuque, Iowa   Madison, Wisconsin
New York, New York   San Francisco, California   St. Louis, Missouri
Bangkok   Bogotá   Caracas   Lisbon   London   Madrid   Mexico City
Milan   New Delhi   Seoul   Singapore   Sydney   Taipei   Toronto

McGraw-Hill

A Division of The McGraw·Hill Companies

Instructor's Manual to accompany
CONNECT WITH ENGLISH: CONVERSATION BOOKS 1-4

2 3 4 5 6 7 8 9 0 QPD QPD 3 2 1 0 9
1 2 3 4 5 6 7 8 9 0 QPD QPD 3 2 1 0 9 8

ISBN 0-07-292759-3

When ordering this title, use ISBN 0-07-115938-X.

http://www.mhhe.com

CONTENTS

INTRODUCTION

CLASSROOM TEACHING SUGGESTIONS FOR THE FOLLOWING EPISODES:

INTRODUCTION

What This Manual Can Do for You

This manual provides essential information on how *Conversation Books 1–4* can be successfully used to help your students improve their oral communication skills in English. This manual tells you:

- what the *Conversation Books* are and what each *Conversation Book* contains;

- how the *Conversation Books* are organized and why they are organized this way;

- the language focus of each activity in the *Conversation Books;*

- how to adjust the level of each activity to match the abilities of your students;

This introduction includes these topics: **a general overview and philosophy** of the books, **chapter organization, classroom management,** and **homework, evaluation and testing.** It is recommended that you read through each of these brief topics, since they will explain the pedagogical principles on which these books are based, including the thematic organization.

In addition, this manual devotes two pages to each individual episode in the section titled *Classroom Teaching Suggestions.* The information you will find there includes:

1. **communicative objectives and language focus** for each activity in the *Conversation Books;*

2. specific suggestions for **how to change the level of the activities** to make them easier for students of lower language proficiency or more challenging for students of higher language proficiency;

3. an **answer key,** for those activities that have definite, right answers.

Finally, the manual has a **testing program,** with oral checklists that cover the main communicative objectives in the books. There is one oral checklist for every four chapters in the books, making twelve checklists in all.

Conversation Books 1–4

There are four *Conversation Books,* each with 12 chapters. Each *Conversation Book* chapter relates to a video episode. Here is how the books are divided:

Book 1   Episodes 1-12
Book 2   Episodes 13-24
Book 3   Episodes 25-36
Book 4   Episodes 37-48

The *Conversation Books* are specifically designed for classroom use. While it is not necessary to have a television and VCR in the classroom, students should watch the corresponding video episode at least once before they attempt the activities in the book. You may assign students to watch the episodes at home, in the library, or in a language lab. Class time can then be spent on completing the activities in the *Conversation Books.*

GENERAL OVERVIEW AND PHILOSOPHY

The purpose of the four *Conversation Books* is to help students develop oral communication skills using the themes found in the **Connect with English** video episodes as a springboard for discussion.

A variety of activities encourages conversation, including role-plays, interviews, surveys, discussions, games, and information gaps. These activities involve the use of common language skills and functions, such as asking for information, expressing opinions, apologizing, congratulating, and so on. (The primary language skills for each activity in the *Conversation Books* are outlined in the *Classroom Teaching Suggestions* section of this manual.)

Using the *Conversation Books,* students engage in natural, authentic conversation. Because the activities are based on themes and issues that arise out of the video episodes, they provide a stimulus — and a natural context — for the exchange of ideas, opinions, and knowledge. For example, in Episode 1, Rebecca talks about her dream of going to music school. The related theme in the *Conversation Book* is called *Pursuing Your Dreams,* and discussion and interview activities encourage students to share their dreams for the future.

The activities in the *Conversation Books* vary in configuration — many are for pairs; a large number are for small or large groups; some are for the entire class. Some activities also involve writing — from simple tasks such as recording one's choices in a list to more sophisticated ones such as writing a paragraph consisting of information gathered from an interview. In this way, the books help promote proficiency not only in speaking and listening, but also in writing and reading.

FLEXIBLE LEVELING

Conversation Books 1–4 are suitable for students at high-beginning through intermediate levels of language proficiency. While the language level and difficulty of the activities have been carefully controlled, the activities in the *Conversation Books* do call for different degrees of language production from students. Some activities may simply require students to ask and answer *yes/no* questions provided in a survey or to make choices from a list or a series of pictures. Others may require more sophisticated use of language, such as arguing one side of an issue or engaging in a multiple-exchange role-play. In other words, the activities vary from ones in which the responses are more controlled to ones that involve free production of English.

To make the material suitable for classes at different levels, the activities can be adjusted to be more or less challenging. In the same way, the material can be adjusted to suit the needs of multilevel classes in which students vary in their language ability.

Special icons are used to identify the difficulty level of each activity in the *Conversation Books*. These icons help teachers tailor the activities for the needs of students at different levels of language proficiency.

- ▲ Arrows pointing up indicate that the difficulty of an activity can be increased.
- ▼ Arrows pointing down indicate the difficulty of an activity can be simplified.
- ⬍ Arrows pointing in both directions indicate that the difficulty level of an activity can be either increased or simplified.

Detailed teaching suggestions for modifying each activity are found in the *Classroom Teaching Suggestions* section of this manual.

CHAPTER ORGANIZATION

Each chapter in the *Conversation Books* is six pages long. In addition, each chapter has a related project found in the Appendices. Here is a summary of the organization of a typical chapter:

• Pages 1–4 COMMUNICATIVE ACTIVITIES

The first four pages of each chapter contain a variety of communicative activities that are based on relevant and important themes derived from the correspondng video episode.

• Pages 5–6 TWO-PAGE ACTIVITY

Pages 5 and 6 of every chapter contain an extended theme that is covered in a two-page activity. These two-page activities alternate among the following:

Games: Games involve students in situations in which they need to use natural language to achieve a specific objective. In many cases, students are directly involved in the creation of game cards or questions. An Appendix in the back of the book also contains game pieces or markers that can be cut out and used as needed.

Information Gaps: For information gaps (controlled pair activities), the material for Student A is on page 5 and the material for Student B is on page 6. Students need to exchange the information they each have in order to complete the activity successfully.

Songs: The song activities are based on the songs that appear within the **Connect with English** story. The songs are also featured on the soundtrack CD or audiocassette.

• Appendix OPTIONAL PROJECT

An optional project for each episode is located in the Appendix. These projects require students to get information outside of class — either through books and other reference sources or through fieldwork, including interviewing people other than their classmates.

*(For more information, refer to the **To the Teacher** and **Visual Tour** sections at the start of each Conversation Book.)*

It is important to note that the activities in an episode are independent. They can be done in any order — so, for example, the two-page game may be the first activity that the class does in a chapter. Occasionally, one or two activities are linked, in which case they should be done in combination. For example, in the first activity, students might be asked to complete a survey. In the following activity they must analyze and report the survey results.

Each activity in the *Conversation Books* is clearly identified by an activity bar, which contains the following information:

- the activity number (by sequence in a chapter);
- the classroom configuration (partner, group, team, class);
- the activity type (e.g., survey, interview, discussion).

There are generally two *What About You?* activities in each chapter. These are a series of two to four questions that prompt students to examine and discuss how a particular theme relates to their lives. The *What About You?* questions can be used as the springboard for whole-class discussions or for students to answer in groups or in pairs. They can even be used for written assignments. These questions are most appropriate for students at higher levels of language proficiency since they often stimulate sophisticated discussions.

Another regular activity type in the *Conversation Books* is called *Ways to Say It*. In these activities, students are introduced to common phrases in English and are provided with situations as prompts to use the phrases in more controlled speaking activities.

PROJECT ACTIVITIES

The project activities are optional and are found in the Appendices located at the back of each of the *Conversation Books*. Project pages contain research-oriented activities or community surveys and polls based on important themes from each episode. The projects reinforce the communicative nature of the books and invite students to expand their learning and conversation beyond the classroom.

For research projects, encourage the use of English-language sources. If possible, see that the students have access to books that are written at a simple level of English and that are well illustrated (these can often be found in the children's section of libraries or bookstores). For fieldwork projects, if the materials are being used in a non-English-speaking environment, students can do the research in the local language but report the results in English. Note that the *Classroom Teaching Suggestions* section of this Instructor's Manual contains many ideas for simplifying the project activities.

CLASSROOM MANAGEMENT

Conversation Books 1–4 are extremely flexible. They can serve as the main text for any course that emphasizes oral communication skills. They can also be used in conjunction with other books in the **Connect with English** print program to create a more comprehensive course that focuses on a wider range of skills. See the section titled **Connect with English** Print Program for more information.

GROUPING

Activities in the *Conversation Books* are designed for a variety of classroom configurations: partner, group, team, class. The type of classroom configuration for each activity is suggested in the corresponding activity bar. Spaces to the right of the activity bars allow students to indicate partner's name, group number, and team number. This makes it easier for students and teachers to keep track of student collaborations. Group and team numbers are also useful when different groups are asked to compare and contrast survey or discussion results with one another.

There are several ways to assign students to pairs, groups, or teams, and you will want to use a variety of approaches:

- A simple way to assign students is to have them count off — even numbers go to one team or group and odd to another.

- Write numbers or letters on small pieces of paper and have students draw them at random. Students are assigned to a team/group according to the number or letter they draw.

- In certain cases, you may want to group students by language proficiency level. For example, a student at a higher proficiency level can be paired with a student at a lower proficiency level. This way the lower-level student can benefit from help from the higher-level student. The same arrangement can be pursued with groups.

- Finally, you might consider grouping students of similar proficiencies. The *Classroom Teaching Suggestions* section of this manual provides alternate activities that can be assigned to different groups within a class according to their ability.

TIMING

The time length for any activity can vary, depending on how much time is devoted to preparation and how much follow-up is done. The *Classroom Teaching Suggestions* section gives a time that typically would be needed for each activity. However, this can be increased if suggested activities in that section are used. Also, the time may be extended if teacher/student modeling is done before students do the activity in their pairs or groups or if follow-up and extension activities are done.

In some cases, students may be particularly interested in a topic and may want to discuss it further. Such student participation and involvement should be encouraged. In other cases, where students are less interested in a topic, you may want to move to another activity on a different theme.

SEQUENCING THE ORDER OF ACTIVITIES

As previously mentioned, any and all of the activities in a chapter can be assigned. In general, all activities are independent of one another—that is, activities can be done in any sequence, or certain activities can be omitted. However, there are some cases where students use information gathered in one activity in a follow-up activity on the same theme.

You may want to consider reviewing and assigning the optional project as students begin work in a unit. This way, by the time the activities in the main chapter are completed, students will be ready to report on their research or fieldwork. Also consider having students play any of the two-page games at the start of each chapter. If this is done, students can play the game several times throughout the course of the chapter.

HOMEWORK, EVALUATION, AND TESTING

HOMEWORK

Most of the activities in the *Conversation Books* are designed as pair and group work, rather than independent work. However, they can be extended in various ways to provide independent work that can be done as homework. Here are some general suggestions:

- Students can answer the *What About You?* questions in writing. They can write short sentences, simple paragraphs, or longer essays.

- Students can write about their personal experiences on any theme once they have completed the related activities in that chapter. For example, after students have finished activities related to the theme of *Best Friends*, they can write about how they met their best friend.

- Students can complete related vocabulary activities. An example of this would be in Activity 1 of Episode 2. Here, students can list and categorize foods in addition to those already provided.

- Students can write word webs related to a theme (see Episode 2, page 3).

- Students can write short summaries of various things such as class debates, interviews, survey results, or even the events in the video episode.

EVALUATION

Given the oral nature of these books, an effective way to judge student achievement and progress is by on-going classroom observation. One way to do this is to have a list of student names next to which to you can make comments as you observe students working in class. You may want to do this once or twice a week. (A reproducible *Notes* section for this purpose can be found at the end of this manual.)

It is also useful for students to do self-evaluations in which they analyze what they have learned. For example, at the end of each episode, students can complete the following sentences:

In this episode, two things I learned are _____

_____.

Now I can _____

_____.

The most interesting thing for me in this episode was _____

_____.

TESTING

In addition to the general suggestions for evaluation mentioned above, twelve oral evaluation checklists are also included in this manual. These oral checklists test the language proficiencies that students have practiced throughout the chapters in the *Conversation Books*. There is one checklist for every four episodes (Episodes 1–4, 5–8, 8–12, etc.).

The oral checklists provide a series of situations that naturally engage students in conversation and elicit the language functions covered in the **Connect with English** episodes. Students will be talking about the themes and situations that have become familiar to them through watching the video episodes and completing the related activities in each chapter. The open-ended answer style allows students of varying proficiencies to demonstrate their individual understanding of the language function and theme.

The oral checklists are relatively short and can be done before, during, or after class. Scores are based on your assessment of a student's proficiency, fluency, and depth of response for each objective. As more objectives are covered, the checklists can provide a general picture both of a student's proficiency as well as a student's progress in using English. (See the introduction to the oral evaluation checklists for more information about scoring.) The checklists can be used as a basis for grading, and can also be placed in a student's portfolio to show progress and work performed.

The *Connect with English* Print Program

CORE COMPONENTS

The *Connect with English* program contains many flexible print materials for a variety of instructional needs. In addition to the three core components — *Video Comprehension Books 1–4, Conversation Books 1–4,* and *Grammar Guides 1–4* — there is a diverse collection of supplemental materials that enhance and enrich the *Connect with English* experience.

VIDEO COMPREHENSION BOOKS 1–4

The *Video Comprehension Books* help students build listening comprehension skills and gain a clear understanding of the characters and story lines found in the *Connect with English* video series. Recognition skills related to facial expressions, body language, and cultural nuances are also emphasized in the exercises which include multiple choice, true/false, sentence completion, and cloze activities. Special *What About You?* activities invite students to share their own opinions and ideas as they relate to the events in the video episode. Additional skills and topics that are covered in each book include reading, oral communication, and vocabulary development.

Using the video with the Video Comprehension Books: Depending on the time and length of the course, instructors may choose to show the *Connect with English* video during class, while simultaneously using the book. However, if repeated access to a television and VCR is not possible, teachers can have their students watch the video episodes in a library, language lab, or at home. Class time can then be used for discussion and review of the activities in the book.

CONVERSATION BOOKS 1-4

Designed specifically for classroom use, the *Conversation Books* help students develop oral communication skills. Each chapter features a variety of communicative partner, group, team, and whole-class activities that provide a natural extension of the themes found in the corresponding video episodes. Activity types vary in each chapter, but generally include an assortment of role-plays, discussions, interviews, surveys, games, information gaps, and questionnaires. Icons indicating the difficulty of each activity allow teachers to adjust the level according to the needs of his/her students. An

optional research project for each episode is found in an Appendix at the back of the book. These projects serve to extend and expand the relevant themes of each chapter as they engage students' interest and involvement in gathering relevant data outside the classroom.

Using the video with the Conversation Books: It is not necessary to have classroom access to the video in order for students to complete the activities in the *Conversation Books.* The activities in these books are based on important themes from the *Connect with English* story. Students are never asked to recall specific information from the corresponding video episode. Instead, they are asked to react, interact, and talk about the story themes and how these themes relate to their own lives. While it is assumed that students will have seen the episode in its entirety at least one time, students' actual viewing can take place either in class, or in a library, language lab, or at home.

GRAMMAR GUIDES 1–4

The *Grammar Guides* assist students in developing mastery of the grammatical structures and vocabulary items found throughout the *Connect with English* video. The topics presented in these four books follow a developmental scope and sequence. Grammatical structures are linked to specific episodes, providing students with contextualized examples. Exercises build from a receptive understanding of the grammar point, to language production through controlled exercises, and finally to *Power Practice* sections in which students write about more personalized, open-ended topics.

Using the video with the Grammar Guides: Students can use the *Grammar Guides* either before or after they watch the corresponding video episode, to either preview or review critical structures and grammatical topics. Lower-level students will find the *Grammar Guides* a valuable resource tool they can rely on to help them internalize the authentic language of the video. More advanced students will welcome the carefully sequenced review of the language and its connection to the video through numerous examples and practice exercises.

SUPPLEMENTAL MATERIALS

CONNECTIONS READERS

The 16 titles in this series of graded readers feature controlled vocabulary and grammar at four distinct levels of difficulty to help students read with understanding as well as enjoyment. (The structures used in the four levels of these readers correspond with the scope and sequence presented in the *Grammar Guides.*)The stories increase in complexity from level to level. The four Level One readers feature exactly the same story found in the video program, told in simplified English and extensively illustrated with color photos. The same basic story is expanded upon in Level Two, only with more reliance on narrative speech. Finally, the Level Three and Four readers dramatically expand the video story line, using the same characters from the video, but putting them in new situations.

VIDEO SCRIPTS 1–4
The scripts for the *Connect with English* video are avail-

able in four separate books, and can be used in conjunction with any of the other materials in the print package. Each script contains the exact dialogue from the video, as well as the stage directions used during the filming of the series. Lines are numbered sequentially throughout the episodes, providing an easy reference for both students and teachers. The *Video Scripts* can be used before, during, or after viewing each episode, for previewing, scanning, and discussion purposes. The scripts are extremely helpful in staging class role-plays, script readings, or even short plays. The scripts also serve as a reference for teachers who wish to concentrate on specific language or grammatical patterns as they appear within the context of the natural language in the video episodes.

HOME VIEWER'S GUIDE

Primarily designed for the self-study audience, the *Home Viewer's Guide* provides a comprehensive review of the entire 48-episode program. Each chapter contains video comprehension exercises, readings on United States' and Canadian culture, and *Behind the Scenes* information about the filming of **Connect with English.** The *Home Viewer's Guide* comes in various bilingual editions including Spanish/English, Mandarin/English, Korean/English, and Thai/English.

CONNECT WITH ENGLISH SOUNDTRACK

The complete soundtrack from the **Connect with English** program is available on CD or audiocassette. It features 12 original songs in a wide range of musical genres including pop, country, jazz, blues, and rap.

FOR INSTRUCTORS

VIDEO COMPREHENSION BOOKS 1–4 INSTRUCTOR'S MANUAL

Over 1000 additional *What About You?* questions and 100 expansion activities provide an abundance of extra options for teachers to choose from. These questions and activities help teachers expand the focus of the class to include speaking, critical thinking, interviews, projects, presentations, and writing assignments. In addition, the range of activities supplied in this manual allows teachers to easily adjust the level of their class to meet students' individual needs. Finally, twelve tests and an answer key provide a comprehensive review of all 48 episodes.

CONVERSATION BOOKS 1–4 INSTRUCTOR'S MANUAL

This manual contains specific teaching suggestions that enable instructors to adjust the level of every activity each of the four books. Also included are oral proficiency checklists that instructors can use as an evaluative device in measuring students' communicative progress.

GRAMMAR GUIDES 1–4 INSTRUCTOR'S MANUAL

Within this manual, teachers will find *Writing with Grammar* and *Communicating with Grammar* activities that provide additional practice with the grammar topics found in each episode. Also included is a detailed answer key.

DISTANCE-LEARNING FACULTY GUIDE

This guide contains useful information about how to use *Connect with English* materials in a distance-learning course, and also offers suggestions for how to establish new credit or non-credit distance-learning programs into any existing ESL/EFL curriculum.

DEMONSTRATION VIDEO

This video contains actual classroom examples of how the *Connect with English* materials can be used in a variety of different instructional settings.

Course options for using the *Connect with English* materials

The **Connect with English** print program is highly flexible and allows instructors to mix and match texts specifically according to their curriculum objectives and student needs. Multi-skills courses may include the use of all three core texts - the *Video Comprehension Books, Conversation Books,* and *Grammar Guides.* For courses with an emphasis on specific skills, many options are possible including those listed below. Of course, this list is by no means exhaustive, as the general design and nature of the entire **Connect with English** program lends itself to a variety of creative and useful classroom applications.

FOR COURSES WITH AN EMPHASIS ON LISTENING COMPREHENSION AND/OR READING AND WRITING:

Of all the core texts, *Video Comprehension Books 1–4* provide the most complete practice in listening comprehension skills. Special *Before You Watch, While You Watch,* and *After You Watch* activities help students understand the general as well as detailed events from the video story. Multiple choice and cloze activities provide practice in reading, and the many *What About You?* questions can be used as writing assignments.

For teachers who wish to incorporate even more reading practice into their course, the *Connections Readers* nicely supplement the *Video Comprehension Books.* They provide an additional source of reading material that ties in directly to the characters and events in the **Connect with English** story. The *Video Scripts* also are valuable components to use for a focus on reading skills. The scripts contain the actual dialogue of each episode, and can provide a great amount of support for students who need help in following the story.

FOR COURSES WITH AN EMPHASIS ON CONVERSATION AND SPEAKING:

Conversation Books 1–4 offer an abundance of practice in conversational skills. Each book contains a variety of partner, group, team, and whole-class activities based on important themes from each episode. Students using these books will also practice reading, writing, listening, and vocabulary skills. The *Conversation Books* pair nicely with the *Video Comprehension Books,* providing students with both communicative practice and a comprehensive review of the events in each episode.

FOR COURSES WITH AN EMPHASIS ON GRAMMAR :

Grammar Guides 1–4 provide a systematic presentation of the basic structures and grammatical features of American English. Each grammar topic is presented in clear and simple charts, and examples from the video episodes are used to highlight these key concepts. The *Grammar Guides* work well when combined with the *Video Comprehension Books* for a complete review of story highlights and an emphasis on grammatical features. In addition, the *Connections Readers* use the same grammatical scope and sequence as the *Grammar Guides,* thereby providing valuable recycling of the featured structures.

CLASSROOM TEACHING SUGGESTIONS

This section provides useful material for using the *Conversation Books* in the classroom.

For each activity, there is:
- a description of the principal language functions (skills) students will demonstrate;
- estimated time required to complete the activity;
- suggestions for adjusting the activity for students of lower and higher language proficiency.

The teaching suggestions on the following pages correspond to the icons found in activity bar preceding each activity in the *Conversation Books:*

▲ *Up:* Arrows pointing up indicate suggestions for how the difficulty or an activity can be **increased.**

▼ *Down:* Arrows pointing down indicate suggestions for how the difficulty of an activity can be **simplified.**

⬍ *Up and Down:* Arrows pointing in both directions indicate suggestions for how the difficulty of an activity can either be **increased or simplified.**

Some activities have additional classroom tips which include such things as suggestions for materials needed or extra follow-up work related to the activity. For those activities with definite answers, an Answer Key is also provided.

E P I S O D E
1
REBECCA'S DREAM

THEME Favorite Songs

| 1 | GROUP | SURVEY | ▲ |

Language Focus: Using vocabulary related to music and musical styles, discussing music, discussing preferences
Classroom Tip: After the activity is finished, have groups report results and add up the votes to find overall results for the class.
Time: 15-20 minutes

ADJUSTING THE LEVEL
Up: Have students work in groups and make a chart like the following for two or three musical types, filling in as much as they can.

MUSICAL TYPE

Songs	
Singers	
Composers	
Instruments	
History/Beginnings	
Interesting Facts	

| 2 | PARTNER | DISCUSSION | ↕ |

Language Focus: Stating preferences in music
Time: 15 minutes

ADJUSTING THE LEVEL
Down: Before pairs do the activity, invite students as a class to give examples of songs and singers in each of the musical categories in Activity 1. Write the names on the board. Have volunteers discuss their favorites from those on the board. As students do the activity, go around and assist with the spelling of proper names.

Up: As a follow-up, have students bring in examples of one or two of their favorite songs in English and play them for the class. Have them talk about the singer, song, style, and the meaning of the lyrics.

THEME Pursuing Your Dreams

| 3 | GROUP | DISCUSSION | ↕ |

Language Focus: Talking about one's personal dreams and plans
Time: 20-30 minutes

ADJUSTING THE LEVEL
Down: Before students do the activity, discuss common "dreams" that people have. Start the discussion by talking about Rebecca's dream to go to music school and be a song-writer and Matt's dream to get married and have children. List dreams on the board.

Up: As a follow-up, have students write a brief paragraph about their dream. They can share their paragraphs with students from a different group.

| 4 | PARTNER | INTERVIEW | ▼ |

Language Focus: Talking about one's personal dreams and plans, discussing options, interviewing
Time: 15-20 minutes

ADJUSTING THE LEVEL
Down: Before students do the activity, invite volunteers to tell about their dreams from Activity 3. With the class, brainstorm a list of options to achieve each dream and write them on the board. Have the class vote on the best options.

THEME Male/Female Relationships

| 5 | GROUP | SURVEY | ▼ |

Language Focus: Giving opinions, interviewing
Time: 15-20 minutes

ADJUSTING THE LEVEL
Down: Before students do the activity, list the following items on the board:

> similar interests, similar age, sense of humor, attractive looks, trustworthy, kind, someone who wants children, a good listener

Ask students to rank the items according to what they think is most important in a relationship with someone of the opposite sex, with 1 being the most important item. Then ask students to tell their number-one choice.

| 6 | PARTNER | DATA ANALYSIS | ▼ |

Language Focus: Making comparisons, making generalizations
Time: 15 minutes

ADJUSTING THE LEVEL
Down: To help students make comparisons, as mentioned in the last part of the activity, write the following on the board:

1. Men and women think alike about relationships. Most of our answers are in the middle column.
2. Men and women think differently about relationships. We have more answers in the right and left columns than in the center column.
3. Women want the same things in relationships. They give fewer different answers than men.
4. Men want the same things in relationships. They give fewer different answers than women.

Have pairs state which conclusions are true or false according to the data they have.

Up: After students do the activity, have them work in groups and write down results by answering these questions:

- Do men and women mostly want the same thing in relationships?
- What's most important to men in relationships? What's most important to women?
- What's most important to most people in relationships?

Then have groups present their report to the class.

SONG Traveling Light

| 7 | GROUP | SONG | ÷ |

Language Focus: Using meaning and context to guess English words
Time: 15 minutes
Answer Key: Answers are found on page 6 of the student book.

ADJUSTING THE LEVEL
Down: Write the missing words from the song on the board. Tell students to find their definitions at the right and then fill them in the blanks in the song.

Up: After students do the activity, have groups discuss the meaning of the song and write a two-sentence summary of it. Then ask students to share any personal experiences they have that relate to the song.

| 8 | PARTNER | WRITING A SONG | ▼ |

Language Focus: Writing a song
Classroom Tip: If possible, you may want to replay the part of the video with the song or listen to the song on the soundtrack.
Time: 20 minutes

ADJUSTING THE LEVEL
Down: To simplify the task, write the outline for one of the stanzas on the board with words missing (similar to what is done in Activity 7). Fill in words as a class to write a new stanza. Tell students to follow the same procedure with their partners as they write their own stanzas.

PROJECT APPENDIX 1

Choosing a College

| 1 | PARTNER | RANKING | ▲ |

Language Focus: Using vocabulary related to schools, talking about characteristics of schools/universities
Time: 15 minutes

ADJUSTING THE LEVEL
Up: After students do the activity, have the pairs interview each other about their ideal situations for each of the items in Activity 1 (e.g., *What is the ideal class size for you?*). Then they join with another pair and describe their partner's opinions about an ideal school.

| 2 | PARTNER | PRESENTATION | ↕ |

Language Focus: Talking about characteristics of schools/universities
Time: 20 minutes (In addition, students do fieldwork outside of class. You may also want to allow class time for the three teams to prepare their presentations.)

ADJUSTING THE LEVEL
Down: Get a college catalog. Explain its setup by showing the table of contents. Put pages with relevant information (e.g., tuition, courses offered, facilities) on overheads and help students find the information useful for the activity. Provide help with vocabulary.

Up: As students do their research, have them find out about as many of the items listed in Activity 1 as they can. Have them include this information in their presentation. Also have them make a list of five advantages of their school in their team presentation. The presentations should be judged on their thoroughness by Team 4.

E P I S O D E 2

DIFFERENCES

THEME Making a Shopping List

1 PARTNER INTERVIEW ▲

Language Focus: Using vocabulary for foods, interviewing
Time: 10-15 minutes

ADJUSTING THE LEVEL

Up: As a follow-up, have pairs play a game. Give pairs a time limit of 15 minutes to categorize the foods pictured (e.g., meat, fruit and vegetables, breads, dairy products) and add as many foods to each category as they can. The pair with the most items in correct categories wins.

As a fieldwork activity, have pairs write a "consumer report" of food stores. Have them compare five of the items in Activity 1 in stores in the area on the following: price, variety (how many different brands there are), and availability (if the product is usually on the shelves). Ask students to put their findings in charts with the three headings (Price, Variety, Availability) and draw conclusions about the best places to shop.

2 GROUP DISCUSSION ⬍

Language Focus: Talking about foods, making plans, negotiating
Time: 20 minutes

ADJUSTING THE LEVEL

Down: To simplify the activity, tell students to choose from the items in Activity 1.

Up: To make the activity more challenging, set a limit for the amount of money groups can spend. List at least 12 food items suitable for parties, and give their prices, including information on quantity (price per unit). Ask students to choose six items, taking into consideration the quantity they need for their party and the price.

THEME Taking Care of Someone

3 CLASS SURVEY ▲

Language Focus: Talking about household activities, giving personal information, interviewing
Time: 20 minutes
Answer Key: a. 4, b. 1, c. 7, d. 8, e. 5, f. 3, g. 2, h. 6

ADJUSTING THE LEVEL

Up: After students do the activity, have each student do a follow-up interview with someone on their list. The student can ask these questions:
- Who is the person you help?
- How often do you help the person?
- How long have you helped the person?
- Why do you help the person?

Then each student writes a brief paragraph about what he/she found out. Students can share their paragraphs in small groups.

4 GROUP DEBATE ▼

Language Focus: Expressing opinions, giving reasons to support an opinion
Time: 20 minutes

ADJUSTING THE LEVEL

Down: To help students think of reasons, suggest that the groups try to complete lists like the following:

Reasons for Rebecca to do (or not to do) work:
She has a full-time job.

Reasons for Kevin to do (or not to do) work:
He gets home from school early and has more time.

Reasons for Mr. Casey to do (or not to do) work:
He is home all day and has more time.

Circulate among the groups, and help students come up with a variety of reasons.

THEME Friendship

5 CLASS DISCUSSION ⬍

Language Focus: Expressing opinions, describing an abstract idea with concrete details
Time: 10 minutes

ADJUSTING THE LEVEL

Down: Before students do the activity, talk about some of your own ideas about friendships, giving examples from some of your own friends.

Up: Before the activity is done as a class, have students work in pairs and come up with their own lists, which they then share with the class.

6 PARTNER FRIENDSHIP TEST ⬍

Language Focus: Talking about oneself
Time: 20 minutes

ADJUSTING THE LEVEL

Down: Before students do the activity, review key vocabulary in the test by writing the following on the board. Ask them to match the words at the left with the definitions at the right.

1. mean (person)   a. with a lot to do
2. busy   b. do well
3. honest   c. telling the truth
4. succeed   d. say you are sorry
5. apologize   e. not nice

Up: Have pairs discuss which two qualities in the test are the most important and why. Have each pair share opinions with another pair.

Then have each student write a paragraph about his/her best friend. Students should try to answer the question: *What qualities (in the test) does my friend have?* Students can share their paragraphs in small groups.

INFORMATION GAP **Saving Money**

| 7 | PARTNER | INFORMATION GAP | ⬍ |

Language Focus: Using vocabulary for investments, asking for and giving information
Classroom Tip: You may want to have available information on different types of investments, such as ads or brochures from banks with rates and information from brokerage firms.
Time: 10 minutes

ADJUSTING THE LEVEL
Down: Before students do the activity, discuss the four types of investments: *savings accounts, certificates of deposit, mutual funds,* and *stock,* writing their names on the board. Then have students use dictionaries to find information on each and on the following terms: *investment, interest rate, savings account.* If possible, show the following on overheads: stock market listings, brochures from banks on rates for savings and CDs, and prospectuses for mutual funds. The purpose is to further help students understand the nature of each type of investment. Ask students to predict the rate for each type of investment and say which types they think are safer.

Up: As a follow-up, tell students to find some information on one type of investment (brochures from banks or mutual funds or applications for saving accounts), bring it to class, and discuss its contents in small groups. Then, as a class, list the advantages and disadvantages of each type of investment.

| 8 | PARTNER | GAME | ⬍ |

Language Focus: Discussing reasons, discussing finances
Time: 10 minutes

ADJUSTING THE LEVEL
Down: Tell pairs to recall the dreams that people have (discussed in Episode 1) as a way to think of reasons to save.

Up: As a follow-up, tell students to interview three or four people (inside or outside class) about ways to save money. Students can use the following questions:
- Do you try to save money?
- Why do you save money?
- What are good ways to save money?

Working in a Factory

| 1 | GROUP | RESEARCH | ▼ |

Language Focus: Using vocabulary related to factories and products, using various sources to get information
Classroom Tip: Have available sources of information that students can use in the project, such as phone books and information about the local chamber of commerce. Once the reserach is done, have groups compare answers.
Time: 10 minutes (In addition, students do fieldwork outside of class. You might want to allow 10-15 minutes of class time for groups to report results.)

ADJUSTING THE LEVEL
Down: Go over sources of information with the class, such as the telephone book. Also, suggest the following: (1) tell students to think of factories/businesses they pass on their way to school and (2) help students find the phone number of a local chamber of commerce (if there is one) to get information.

| 2 | GROUP | FACTORY INTERVIEW | ▼ |

Language Focus: Getting information, using interview skills
Classroom Tip: Have groups report the information they obtain to the class.
Time: 10 minutes (In addition, students do fieldwork outside of class. You may want to allow 15-30 minutes of class time for groups to report results.)

ADJUSTING THE LEVEL
Down: Work directly with the students in making contacts with the factories and setting up people for them to interview. If groups are going to do interviews in factories, it would be a good idea to invite a guest speaker to class for groups to practice their interview skills before they go off on their own.

Finally, discuss ways for students to record their interview, such as in a notebook or on tape (if the person being interviewed grants such permission). Also, consider dividing up the interview questions among the students.

EPISODE 3

A VISIT TO THE DOCTOR

THEME Going to the Doctor

1 GROUP CATEGORIES ▲

Language Focus: Using vocabulary related to medicine
Time: 15 minutes
Answer Key: Things the doctor uses: needle, X-ray, scale, stethoscope; *Things you do at the doctor's:* take off your clothes, open your mouth and say "AHH," get a shot, explain how you're feeling; *People who work at the doctor's office:* doctor, lab technician, receptionist, nurse; *Things the doctor does:* checks your blood pressure, writes a prescription, listens to your heart, checks your temperature

ADJUSTING THE LEVEL

Up: As a follow-up, give each group a large piece of paper. Have each make a word web (series of circles connected by lines) related to a doctor's visit. (See Episode 2, page 3, for an example of a web). Have students start with a circle with the words *Doctor's visit* in the center. They then write categories from the activity in smaller circles, as well as the following: *Things you see in a doctor's office, Tests you take at a doctor's office, Medicine.* Students add words for each category by drawing lines from the circle and writing them on the lines (e.g., *medicine* could be related to terms such as *pills, dosage, pharmacist*). Students can use dictionaries for the activity. Have groups share their webs with the class, discussing the meaning of words.

Then have group members discuss their last visit to a doctor for a checkup and encourage them to use the words from their webs.

2 PARTNER INTERVIEW ▲

Language Focus: Telling about one's personal experiences, interviewing
Time: 10 minutes

ADJUSTING THE LEVEL

Up: Have students work in their groups from Activity 1 and give their opinions about the items in the chart, telling whether they are good or bad and why.

> EXAMPLE
> • It is good to go to the doctor with someone. The other person can help you feel less nervous.

> • It is good to ask the doctor a lot of questions. You want to have all the information you need about your health.

Then have students make a list of ten pieces of health advice about going to the doctor.

> EXAMPLE
> • You should go to the doctor at least once a year.
> • You should find a doctor you feel comfortable talking with.

THEME Career Choices

3 PARTNER COMPARE OPINIONS ↕

Language Focus: Using words for occupations, talking about jobs, giving opinions, interviewing
Classroom Tip: After the activity is finished, have pairs report results and make a list on the board of the class's ideas about the best and worst jobs.
Time: 10-15 minutes

ADJUSTING THE LEVEL

Down: Before students do the activity, have volunteers explain what people in each job do and name some of the advantages and disadvantages of each job.

> EXAMPLE
> *Firefighter*
> *Job:* puts out fires, teaches fire safety, takes care of fire engines
> *Advantages:* helps people, can save lives, has a lot of time off work, makes a good salary, has good benefits
> *Disadvantages:* work is dangerous and stressful, can spend a lot of time waiting

Up: As a follow-up, have pairs list the advantages and disadvantages of each job. Have several pairs join together and compare their opinions about the jobs, as well as their lists.

4 CLASS GAME ↕

Language Focus: Using vocabulary for occupations
Time: 15-20 minutes

ADJUSTING THE LEVEL

Down: Before students do the activity, have them work in groups and try to list at least two jobs that begin with each letter of the alphabet. They should not look at these lists when they do the activity.

Up: After students do the activity, have them do the following variation: Each adds a sentence about what Kevin will do in the job.

> EXAMPLE
> • Kevin will be an actor. He will act in plays onstage.
> • Kevin will be a banker. He will give people loans to open businesses.

| 5 | TEAM | PUZZLE | ▲ |

Language Focus: Using vocabulary for food
Time: 5 minutes
Answer Key: 1. Rick, 2. Tim, 3. Connie, 4. Kim, 5. Joan

ADJUSTING THE LEVEL
Up: Have students work in groups of five and role-play planning what they will each bring to a barbecue. One student acts as a leader and tries to make sure that there is a variety of food for the barbecue.

| 6 | PARTNER | INTERVIEW | ▲ |

Language Focus: Using vocabulary for food, discussing customs/culture, interviewing
Time: 10-15 minutes

ADJUSTING THE LEVEL
Up: Have students work in groups and list foods that they know are popular with Americans. Have group members take a tally of which foods they have tried.

Have individual students make lists of the ingredients for each of the foods on the list. Encourage them to use cookbooks to check their lists.

> EXAMPLE
> brownies: butter, chocolate, eggs, salt, sugar, vanilla, flour, nuts (pecans)

GAME **What's Your Job?**

| 7 | TEAM | GAME | ◆ |

Language Focus: Asking questions, discussing what people do in their jobs

ADJUSTING THE LEVEL
Down: Before students do the activity, model it. Choose an occupation such as journalist or computer programmer without telling the students what you have chosen. Have individual students ask you the questions in the book, as well as some of their own, in order to guess the occupation.

Up: After students play the game in the activity, have them play this variation. Have students work in pairs. Write the numbers from 1-36 on slips of paper and have pairs choose two slips at random. Each pair has three minutes to write as many ways as they can think of in which the jobs are alike.

Students write a paragraph about which job they would like best and why. Post students' paragraphs for other students to read.

Holidays

| 1 | GROUP | RESEARCH | ◆ |

Language Focus: Getting information from English-language sources and reporting results, discussing customs/culture
Classroom Tip: You may want to have available books about American holidays. These can be written in fairly simple English, such as those intended for children. Illustrated books would be especially useful for this activity.

In addition, you may want to provide students with materials to make posters, such as large sheets of paper.
Time: 20-30 minutes (In addition, students do research outside of class.)

ADJUSTING THE LEVEL
Down: Provide students with sources in simple language, as mentioned above. In addition, have students interview you in class regarding one or two of the holidays, using the questions.

You may want groups to present their reports to you before they present them to the class. You can give suggestions or ask questions to help groups improve their reports.

Up: Ask students to come up with two or three additional questions to answer about the holiday. Groups then answer them as well.

| 2 | GROUP | RESEARCH | ◆ |

Language Focus: Using various sources to get information, using interview skills, discussing customs/culture
Time: 20 minutes (In addition, students do research outside of class.)

ADJUSTING THE LEVEL
Down: Before students begin the activity, brainstorm, as a class, holidays to include. Encourage students to talk about holidays in their cultures.

Up: Have groups write a brief paragraph about each holiday, in addition to filling in the chart. Each group member might be assigned one or two holidays to write about.

E P I S O D E
4
CELEBRATIONS

THEME Expressing Congratulations

1 | PARTNER | DISCUSSION ▲

Language Focus: Expressing congratulations, discussing important life events
Time: 15 minutes
Answer Key: 1. a birthday, 2. a new job, 3. a wedding, 4. a new baby, 5. a new home

ADJUSTING THE LEVEL
Up: After students do the activity, have pairs discuss three or four events for which they received congratulations and tell why. Then they each should choose one of their events and write a brief paragraph about it. Have two pairs get together and share paragraphs.

2 | GROUP | WAYS TO SAY IT ⬍

Language Focus: Expressing congratulations
Time: 20 minutes

ADJUSTING THE LEVEL
Down: Before students do the role-play, go over the expressions of congratulations with the class. Then select situations from Activity 1 and have students respond first in groups and then individually, using the expressions.
> EXAMPLE
> T: I just bought a new house.
> Ss: That's wonderful!

Finally, have pairs of volunteers do similar exchanges in front of class.

Up: Have students extend the role-plays they present to at least six to eight exchanges. For example, the student hearing the news about a new house can ask for more information, such as the size of the house and where it is located.

THEME Graduation from High School

3 | PARTNER | INTERVIEW ▲

Language Focus: Talking about customs/culture, using vocabulary related to graduation from school, interviewing
Classroom Tip: Bring to class examples or pictures of items mentioned, such as diplomas, yearbook, and cap and gown.
Time: 15 minutes

ADJUSTING THE LEVEL
Up: Extend the activity by having students ask a follow-up question for each *yes* answer.
> EXAMPLE
> What are the *diplomas* like?

Then partners tell each other about graduations in their schools. Each partner should repeat back as much as he/she can remember about his/her partner's graduation.

4 | PARTNER | DISCUSSION ▼

Language Focus: Talking about customs/culture
Time: 15 minutes

ADJUSTING THE LEVEL
Down: Before students do the activity, brainstorm a list of traditional graduation activities with the class and write the list on the board. Guide the discussion by including information from your own high school and your knowledge of high schools in the United States.

As a follow-up to the activity, have pairs share information with other pairs, telling how their graduations were alike and how they were different.

THEME Getting Accepted

5 | TEAM | GAME ⬍

Language Focus: Describing reactions to good news
Time: 15-20 minutes

ADJUSTING THE LEVEL
Down: Before students do the activity, have them work in pairs and discuss the ways people react to good news. Try to pair students of lower and higher language proficiency for this preparation activity. Tell them to discuss this question:
> You receive the news that you have gotten a good job that pays you twice as much money as your current job. What do you do?

Tell students to brainstorm a variety of responses, as well as giving their own personal responses.

Up: Have students work in groups of three or four and write a script about a person who receives good news about any topic of their choice. They should include what the person does and says as he/she talks to people that day. Have the groups perform their skits for the class.

6 | PARTNER | STORYTELLING ▼

Language Focus: Describing a situation, telling stories
Time: 20-30 minutes

ADJUSTING THE LEVEL
Down: Guide students' storytelling by writing the following questions on the board and suggesting that they answer them in their stories:

- Who is the person? What's his name?
- Why is he waiting for the call?
- How does he feel when he's waiting for the call?
- What news does he get over the phone?
- What does the person on the other end of the phone say?
- What does he say in response?
- How does he feel at the end?
- What is he going to do next?

INFORMATION GAP
Different Types of Families

7	PARTNER	INFORMATION GAP	↕

Language Focus: Practicing vocabulary for family relationships, asking for and giving information
Time: 15-20 minutes
Answer Key:
Part A, page 5: 1. He's dead., 2. She's 66., 3. Sue, 4. Mary, 5. Ben
Part A, page 6: 1. Alice, 2. 44, 3. Bill, 4. Larry, 5. He's adopted.
Part B, both pages: 1. Sue, Rosa, 2. Joe, 3. Bob and Ruth, 4. Tom and Mary, 5. Sue and Joe

ADJUSTING THE LEVEL
Down: Before students do the activity, draw a simple family tree on the board based on the one in the book. Start with Amy and her immediate family, and add on from there. Write in proper names and ages for people in the family, and have students discuss the relationships between people. Discuss the meanings of the words *adopted, divorced, remarried, half-brother.*

Up: After students do the activity, have each pair write five additional questions about Amy's family and ask the questions of another pair.

PROJECT   APPENDIX 4

Being Proud

1	PARTNER	SURVEY	↕

Language Focus: Getting information, asking questions, using interview skills
Time: 10 minutes (In addition, students do fieldwork outside of class. You may want to allow five to ten minutes of class time to explain the activity.)

ADJUSTING THE LEVEL
Down: To model the task, have students ask you the questions before they do their interviews. Students can write down your answers on a separate piece of paper. (Students will use these in Activity 2.)

Up: After they do the task, have students work in groups and share results. Ask them if they find any similarities in the answers people give.

2	PARTNER	WRITING	↕

Language Focus: Writing a paragraph
Time: 20-30 minutes

ADJUSTING THE LEVEL
Down: Model the activity. Have students refer to the notes on the answers you gave (see Activity 1 above, "Adjusting the Level" — *Down* suggestions). Have them choose one from the set of questions. Write a model paragraph on the board, taking suggestions from students on what to include. Model how to write an opening and concluding sentence.

Up: As an extension, have students choose one of the questions in Activity 1, and write their own personal answer to the question. Have students share their paragraphs in small groups.

EPISODE 5

BREAKING THE NEWS

THEME Buying a Used Car

| 1 | TEAM | GAME | ▲ |

Language Focus: Using vocabulary to describe cars
Time: 10 minutes
Answer Key: 1. b, 2. d, 3. e, 4. a, 5. f, 6. c

ADJUSTING THE LEVEL

Up: As a class, list and discuss types of cars, including the ones in the pictures in the activity (e.g., convertible, sports car, truck, van, vintage/antique car).

Present a page of car ads from a newspaper or the Internet on an overhead, or have students bring in their own car ads. Have them work in groups and make a list of unfamiliar words and abbreviations, together with guesses for the meanings of items. Ask groups to share their words and guesses with the class. Supply appropriate definitions or explanations, as needed.

Finally, have groups of students rank the following factors in choosing a car in order of importance: color, speed, price, size, gas mileage.

| 2 | GROUP | DISCUSSION | ▼ |

Language Focus: Using vocabulary to describe cars and optional features, giving opinions, negotiating
Time: 15-20 minutes

ADJUSTING THE LEVEL

Down: Before students do the activity, make a list of features and options on your car or students' cars (e.g., 4-wheel drive, air conditioning, airbags, stereo, automatic shift, 6-cylinder engine, CD player). Write the list on the board. Make sure that the key ones in Activity 2 are on the list. Discuss why it is good to have each feature or option. Invite students to add to your list.

THEME A Shopping Mall

| 3 | PARTNER | INTERVIEW | ▲ |

Language Focus: Using vocabulary related to stores, interviewing
Time: 10-15 minutes

ADJUSTING THE LEVEL

Up: Have pairs ask why questions in their interviews (e.g., *Why do you want to go to that store?, Why don't you want to go to that store?*). They can write answers on a separate piece of paper.

Then have pairs play a game. Have students list all the items that they can buy in each of the first four stores. Give a time limit of ten minutes. The pair with the most correct items wins. Then repeat the game with the last four stores.

THEME Formal and Informal Clothes

| 4 | GROUP | BRAINSTORM | ⬍ |

Language Focus: Practicing vocabulary for clothes
Classroom Tip: Have available additional pictures of clothing to help students with vocabulary. Good sources are picture dictionaries or clothing catalogues.
Time: 10-15 minutes
Answer Key: *Formal clothes:* jacket, tie, high heels, bow tie, skirt, evening gown, tuxedo; *Informal clothes:* sandals, tank top, sweater and leggings, jeans, sneakers, shorts, T-shirt

ADJUSTING THE LEVEL

Down: To prompt students' thinking for additional clothing vocabulary, have available pictures of people in a variety of situations from magazines. Encourage students to use a dictionary for help with finding words and checking their spellings. Also, talk with students about the differences between formal and informal clothing.

Up: As a follow-up, give students a list of situations like the following and have them suggest appropriate clothes for men/women to wear for each:
- a wedding in an elegant hotel
- a wedding in someone's home
- a barbecue/outdoor party at a friend's house
- a beach party
- a birthday dinner at a friend's house
- going to work on an ordinary day
- going to work when you have an important meeting
- going to a party at an elegant restaurant
- going to a party at your friend's house

Have students discuss any differences between what people in the United States would wear and what people in their countries would wear.

| 5 | PARTNER | ROLE-PLAY | ▼ |

Language Focus: Using language related to shopping for clothes, expressing needs/wants, making suggestions
Time: 15-20 minutes

ADJUSTING THE LEVEL

Down: Before students do the activity, go over the list of events in Box A and discuss clothing appropriate for each.

Model a role-play situation with the class. Decide on an event. Decide on appropriate questions for the event. Decide on appropriate clothes or color. Then, as a class, make up a role-play and write it on the board.

EXAMPLE
Situation: a special date
Where is it?: at a fancy restaurant
Appropriate clothes: (woman — dress, man — suit)

Role-Play:
Customer: I need something to wear on a special date.
Salesperson: Where is the date?
Customer: It's at an elegant restaurant.
Salesperson: What about this black dress? It's very elegant.

To help structure the role-plays, tell the student who is the customer to have specific answers to the first three questions. The salesperson then suggests appropriate items of clothing and color based on the information given.

GAME A Parent's Approval

6	TEAM	GAME	⬍

Language Focus: Expressing wants and desires, discussing plans
Classroom Tip: You may want to model the game. Read the items in the Example. Have two groups of two students each write whether Mr. Casey would approve or disapprove and then compare their answers in front of the class.
Time: 20-25 minutes (The game can be replayed several times.)

ADJUSTING THE LEVEL

Down: To make the task of preparing cards easier, have students work in pairs. Try to pair students of lower language proficiency with those of higher proficiency. Members of pairs then play on different teams.

Up: As a follow-up, have students work in pairs and choose two situations: one that people agree Mr. Casey would approve of and one that Mr. Casey would not approve of. Have them role-play both situations, taking the roles of Mr. Casey and Kevin or Rebecca. Kevin and Rebecca say what they want to do and why, and Mr. Casey tells whether or not he approves.

Shopping for Clothes

1	PARTNER	CONSUMER RESEARCH	⬍

Language Focus: Practicing vocabulary for clothing, discussing prices
Classroom Tip: You may want to have some newspapers or clothing catalogues available for students to refer to. Or you may want to arrange for a class trip to a shopping mall or area.
Time: 10-15 minutes (In addition, students do fieldwork outside of class.)

ADJUSTING THE LEVEL

Down: Model doing the activity for yourself. First, make a list of things you need/want. Then look for each of the items in a clothing catalogue or newspaper: find the one you like best for your outfit and the one that is the cheapest. You might prepare overheads, using pages that you have selected in advance.

Up: In addition to writing the name of the item in their charts, have students give a detailed description of the item.
  EXAMPLE
  • Black silk dress with a short skirt and long sleeves, gold sequins around the neck
  • High heels in black suede

2	PARTNER	RESEARCH	▼

Language Focus: Talking about prices, giving opinions
Time: 15-20 minutes

ADJUSTING THE LEVEL

Down: Model how to read various types of exchange rates and make calculations.
  EXAMPLE
  Rate:
  Number of Japanese yen to a U.S. dollar = 130.20
  Calculation:
  $60 X 130.20 = 7812 yen
  $60 = 7,812 yen

EPISODE
6

SAYING GOODBYE

THEME **Saying Goodbye to Friends**

| 1 | PARTNER | WAYS TO SAY IT | ⬍ |

Language Focus: Saying goodbye
Time: 10-15 minutes

ADJUSTING THE LEVEL
Down: Before students do the activity, have them practice saying the expressions in the box. Go over them as a class. Then have a "spelling bee." Put the expressions from Column A on separate pieces of paper. Two students take turns picking from these papers at random and reading the expressions. The other students are standing up. They take turns responding to the expressions. If they cannot give a response, they sit down. The player or players standing at the end are winners.

Up: After students do the activity, have them role-play saying goodbye to Rebecca. They can act out a scene in which they pretend to be either players on her softball team or her co-workers at the factory.

| 2 | GROUP | GOODBYE CARDS | ⬍ |

Language Focus: Using expressions of goodbye, writing expressions of goodbye
Classroom Tip: Have colored markers, pencils, or crayons available for students to make cards. You might also want to have colored paper. It would also be a good idea to show students examples of goodbye cards in English (these could be ones sold commercially or found on the Internet).
Time: 20 minutes

ADJUSTING THE LEVEL
Down: Before students do the activity, present expressions useful for goodbye cards (e.g., *You're going away, but we won't forget you., Don't forget to phone., Good luck in ____.).*

Up: Have students write a note to someone who is going away. It can be either to Rebecca or to someone they know. They should try to include appropriate information, such as where the person is going and how they can keep in touch.

THEME **Music Lessons**

| 3 | TEAM | GAME | ▼ |

Language Focus: Using vocabulary for musical instruments
Time: 10 minutes
Answer Key: Percussion: bongos, drums, xylophone; *Woodwind:* clarinet, flute, saxophone; *Brass:* tuba, trombone, trumpet; *String:* piano, violin, guitar

ADJUSTING THE LEVEL
Down: Go over the names of the instruments before students play the game. Explain the meanings of the categories:
Percussion: instruments you hit
Woodwinds: instruments you blow through a mouth hole
Brass: instruments you blow through a mouthpiece shaped like a cup or funnel
Strings: instruments in which strings move or vibrate
    After students do the activity, discuss how each instrument is played.
    EXAMPLE
    You blow into a tuba.
    You hit the xylophone with sticks.
    You play the strings of a violin with a bow.

| 4 | CLASS | SURVEY | ▲ |

Language Focus: Using vocabulary related to music and musical instruments, giving personal information, interviewing
Time: 15-20 minutes

ADJUSTING THE LEVEL
Up: As part of the survey or as a separate survey, have students ask the following questions:
  • What musical instrument would you like to play? Why?
  • What is your favorite musical instrument?
Have students discuss results as a class, answering the following questions:
  • What instruments would most people like to play?
  • Why is that instrument so popular?

THEME **Junk Food**

| 5 | GROUP | CATEGORIES | ⬍ |

Language Focus: Using vocabulary for food
Time: 10-15 minutes
Answer Key: Note that some foods can go into both the junk food and fast food categories. *Healthy food:* pizza, fruit juice, tofu, fruit, steamed vegetables, broiled fish, herbal tea; *Junk food:* cookies, potato chips, soda, candy; *Fast food:* hot dogs, French fries, hamburgers, milk shakes

ADJUSTING THE LEVEL
Down: Before students do the activity, go over the foods on the list. Ask them which foods they have eaten. If necessary, explain the ingredients of pizza and milk shakes, and the difference between herbal tea and regular tea. Also explain

the differences between cooking methods: *frying, broiling, grilling,* and *steaming.* If necessary, have students refer to a dictionary. Have students discuss which are most healthful.

Finally, brainstorm some possible additional food categories with the class, such as *breakfast foods* or *snack foods.*

Up: Give groups ten minutes to add additional items to each category. Have groups compare and discuss answers.

6 | PARTNER | INTERVIEW ▾

Language Focus: Using vocabulary for food, giving personal information, interviewing, giving advice
Time: 15-20 minutes

ADJUSTING THE LEVEL
Down: Before students do the activity, discuss healthful food versus unhealthful food. For example, have students categorize the following and tell why they chose the category:
  • cake (unhealthful — too much sugar)
  • banana (healthful — fruit with potassium)
  • ice cream (rich in nutrients but also in sugar and fats)
  • fried foods (unhealthful — full of fats)
  • broiled foods (more healthful — low in fats)
  • water (healthful — cleans your cells and tissues)
  • soda (unhealthful — too much sugar)
As partners interview one another, encourage them to help each other with spellings and to use dictionaries. As students do Part C of the activity, they should look for foods that are unhealthful. They should discuss these questions:
  • Are there too many unhealthful foods on the list?
  • Are there enough fruits and vegetables?

INFORMATION GAP   Baseball

7 | PARTNER | INFORMATION GAP ↕

Language Focus: Learning baseball vocabulary, using location words, asking for and giving information
Classroom Tip: Get a diagram of a baseball field to show students. These can be found in encyclopedias.
Time: 20-25 minutes

ADJUSTING THE LEVEL
Down: To help students do the activity, put a diagram of a baseball field on an overhead or draw one on the board. The various positions and parts of the field can be labeled and reviewed.

Up: Have pairs look up the meanings of the following baseball terms in a dictionary and give their definitions: *an inning, an out, a home run, a run, a strike, a pinch-hit.* Also, have students find the meanings of the following idioms:
  • I think that we have <u>covered all of the bases.</u> Our speech for the meeting is ready. We have included all the topics we need to.
  • His ideas are always a little <u>off base.</u> He is a very strange person.
Pairs can compare answers.

PROJECT

The Boston Red Sox

1 | PARTNER | RESEARCH ↕

Language Focus: Using sources to get information, using sports-related language
Classroom Tip: You may want to have current or year-end standings for major league baseball teams available. These can be found in newspapers or on the Internet.
Time: 15-20 minutes (In addition, students do research outside of class.)

ADJUSTING THE LEVEL
Down: Provide students with the standings for the National or American League.

Up: On an outline map of the United States and Canada, have students mark and label the cities that have major league teams, as well as give the team names.
Have students do research to answer these additional baseball questions:
  • How many games do major league teams play a year?
  • When does the baseball season begin and end?
  • What is a good batting average?
  • What is a good number of wins for a pitcher?

2 | GROUP | RESEARCH ▲

Language Focus: Using sports-related language, using sources to get information, reporting information
Time: 20 minutes (In addition, students do research outside of class.)

ADJUSTING THE LEVEL
Up: In addition to the information asked for in the activity, have students find historical information about a team or one or two of its famous players, and share it with the class.

EPISODE 7
LEAVING HOME

THEME Surprises

| 1 | PARTNER | WAYS TO SAY IT | ⇕ |

Language Focus: Expressing surprise, responding to news
Time: 10-15 minutes

ADJUSTING THE LEVEL

Down: Before students do the activity, write the expressions of surprise on the board. Orally present examples of "surprise" news (e.g., *Everyone got a 100 on the test. We are going on a class trip.*). Have students respond orally first in groups and then individually, using the expressions on the board.

Up: Students work in pairs and choose a piece of news (such as winning a prize or seeing a movie star). They make up a role-play of at least six exchanges in which one student tells the news to the other. Then the pairs present the role-plays to the class.

THEME Presents

| 2 | PARTNER | DISCUSSION | ▲ |

Language Focus: Learning vocabulary for common presents, expressing preferences, interviewing
Time: 15 minutes

ADJUSTING THE LEVEL

Up: Have students write a list of five specific items they want (based on those in the activity), and explain why. They can share lists with their partners.

> EXAMPLE
> I want a ticket to the Stars concert next week.
> I want it because the Stars are my favorite musical group.

| 3 | TEAM | GAME | ⇕ |

Language Focus: Practicing vocabulary for jewelry, clothing, sports equipment, entertainment
Classroom Tip: You may want students to use dictionaries as they look for additional words in the various categories.
Time: 20-30 minutes
Answer Key: Jewelry: bracelet, earrings, necklace, ring; *Clothing:* shirts, leather jacket, hat, sneakers; *Things with wheels:* bicycle, in-line skates, motorcycle, skateboard; *Entertainment:* cassette, CD, tickets, video. *Additional items and category will vary.*

ADJUSTING THE LEVEL

Down: To review vocabulary, make an overhead of Activity 2 without the names of the items. Ask students to work in pairs and write the names of the items on a pieces of paper.

Up: Have teams play a continuation of the games. They have ten minutes to brainstorm other categories of presents (e.g., electronic items, food items, and things for the house) and then list several items for each. Teams get five points for each category and one for each item.

| 4 | PARTNER | ROLE-PLAY | ▼ |

Language Focus: Expressing wants and needs, asking for advice, describing items
Time: 15-30 minutes

ADJUSTING THE LEVEL

Down: Model doing the activity. Choose someone for whom to buy a gift — either a character from *Connect with English* or a student in class (e.g., someone whose birthday is soon). Take suggestions from the class and write out a dialogue. Focus on key language for students to repeat and use in their role-plays, such as the language underlined in the example.

> EXAMPLE
> A: I want to buy a present for (my brother).
> B: How old is (he)?
> A: He's 17.
> B: Is it a special occasion?
> A: Yes. He is graduating from high school.
> B: How about a pen? People often give pens for graduation. Here is a beautiful gold one.

To further structure the activity, suggest that students use the items from Activity 2. "Salespeople" have these items available, and "customers" are trying to buy one of the items.

THEME Good Luck/Bad Luck

| 5 | GROUP | DISCUSSION | ▼ |

Language Focus: Talking about customs/culture
Classroom Tip: You may want to bring in examples of items related to luck such as a rabbit's foot or a four-leaf clover.
Time: 10 minutes

ADJUSTING THE LEVEL

Down: Model the activity by talking to the class about items that are good luck or bad luck in the United States and Canada, such as these:

> *Good luck:* a horseshoe, finding a penny
> *Bad luck:* the number 13 (that's why many tall buildings don't have a floor labeled "13"), a black cat, walking under a ladder, opening an umbrella indoors

| **6** | GROUP | OPINION SURVEY | ⬍ |

Language Focus: Interviewing, talking about personal beliefs
Time: 15 minutes

ADJUSTING THE LEVEL

Down: Have students tell the month and day of their birth. Then make a chart like the one in the book and model the activity by asking several volunteers the questions and writing answers.

Up: Have students ask these additional questions and write the answers on a separate piece of paper:
- How old are you?
- Are your parents superstitious?
- What is one thing that means good luck to you?
- What is a superstition that sometimes worries you?

(Students will use these answers in Activity 7.)

| **7** | PARTNER | DISCUSSION | ▲ |

Language Focus: Making comparisons, making generalizations, stating conclusions
Time: 10-15 minutes

ADJUSTING THE LEVEL

Up: Before students do the activity, have them predict the results. After they do the activity, have the class discuss whether the results surprise them.

Then ask students to form groups. Ask them to discuss the following factors and their effect on whether one is superstitious, using the information they have gathered: sex, date of birth, age, parents' beliefs.

GAME
A Trip Across the U.S. with Rebecca

| **8** | TEAM | GAME | ⬍ |

Language Focus: Formulating and asking questions
Time: 30 minutes

ADJUSTING THE LEVEL

Down: Review how to form *Who, What, Where,* and *Why* questions, mentioning the use of *do/does/did* and inversion of *be.* To help students form questions, write several possible answers on the board, and have the class orally brainstorm questions for the answers.

    EXAMPLE
    A: Sandy
    Q: Who is Rebecca's friend?

    A: Because she was leaving for school in San Francisco.
    Q: Why did Rebecca quit her job?

Up: Have students play the game again, writing new questions. This time, students must answer two questions correctly in order to roll again.

Discovering the United States

| **1** | GROUP | RESEARCH | ▲ |

Language Focus: Learning names of geographic locations
Classroom Tip: Have available a large piece of paper and colored pencils or markers for students to make a large map. Present the names for the various regions as you introduce the activity: Northeast, South, Midwest, Northwest, Southwest/West.
Time: 30-40 minutes

ADJUSTING THE LEVEL

Up: Have students put additional information on the class map, such as names of major cities, state capitals, geographical features (mountains, rivers, lakes, etc.), and important sites to visit.

    Play a guessing game with states. Students divide into teams. Choose a state and give clues to describe it one at a time (e.g., *It's in the Midwest. It's south of Wisconsin. Indiana is one of its neighbors.*). Teams get a point for each correct guess but are out of the round if they guess incorrectly. After several rounds, invite volunteers to give clues.

| **2** | PARTNER | STATE RESEARCH | ⬍ |

Language Focus: Getting information from English-language sources, reporting information
Classroom Tip: Have available almanacs and other reference books with geographic information for the United States.
Time: 20 minutes (In addition, students do research outside of class.)

ADJUSTING THE LEVEL

Down: Write the chart from the activity on the board. Show students or read an entry about a state from an almanac. Help students with any unfamiliar vocabulary — either by helping them understand words from context or by using a dictionary. Complete the chart as a class.

Up: Have students present the information they find in the form of a tourist brochure for the area. Tell them to include the facts but also to try to persuade people to come and visit the area.

E P I S O D E

8

THE STRANGER

THEME Talking to Strangers

| 1 | PARTNER | INTERVIEW | ▲ |

Language Focus: Giving opinions, interviewing
Time: 10-15 minutes

ADJUSTING THE LEVEL
Up: Have pairs describe each of the situations orally and have each tell why he or she would or would not talk to the stranger. Ask the pairs to list situations where it would be OK to talk to strangers in their culture. Finally, discuss these questions in class.
- Is it OK to talk to someone sitting next to you on the bus? If yes, when it is OK? Always or just sometimes?
- Is it OK to talk to someone in an elevator? If yes, when is it OK?
- Is it OK to talk to someone of the opposite sex?

| 2 | CLASS | DEBATE | ↕ |

Language Focus: Expressing opinions, giving reasons for opinions
Time: 20-25 minutes

ADJUSTING THE LEVEL
Down: As a lead-in to the activity, have students discuss the situations in Activity 1. Have them talk about situations when it seems OK to trust a stranger and situations when it seems better not to trust a stranger.

Up: Have students do a follow-up round to their debate. After both groups have presented, each group gets three minutes to address the other group's arguments and restate its own strongest reasons.

   After this, have the class discuss the two strongest reasons found for each opinion.

THEME Being Afraid

| 3 | CLASS | GAME | ↕ |

Language Focus: Talking about personal characteristics
Time: 20 minutes

ADJUSTING THE LEVEL
Down: As a lead-in to the activity, have students discuss common fears that people have. You can prompt them with some of the following ideas: fear of heights, fear of being alone in the house, fear of being alone outside after dark, fear of snakes.

Up: As a follow-up, have the class identify the most common and most unusual fears. Then invite volunteers to discuss why they think they have particular fears. Other students can offer advice for overcoming the fear.

| 4 | PARTNER | MATCHING | ▼ |

Language Focus: Analyzing words and word parts
Classroom Tip: Have students use their dictionaries for this activity, or have dictionaries available for students to refer to (these should be dictionaries that have etymologies that will explain the origin and meaning of word parts).
Time: 10-15 minutes
Answer Key: A. 4, B. 6, C. 10, D. 8, E. 9, F. 5, G. 2, H. 3, I. 1, J. 7

ADJUSTING THE LEVEL
Down: Point out that each word at the left in the activity ends in "phobia," which means "fear" and comes from ancient Greek. Tell students to look in a dictionary for the words or look for other words that have the same beginning. (You may want to put an entry with etymology on an overhead and explain how to read it.) They should use the information they find in the dictionary to help them do the matching activity.

| 5 | GROUP | GAME | ▼ |

Language Focus: Understanding and using word parts
Time: 15-20 minutes

ADJUSTING THE LEVEL
Down: To prompt their thinking, ask students to think of things that they don't like and they don't like to do, and invent a phobia related to these things. For example: homeworkophobia.

THEME Car Trouble

| 6 | PARTNER | DISCUSSION | ▲ |

Language Focus: Giving opinions and advice
Time: 10-15 minutes

ADJUSTING THE LEVEL
Up: As partners compare answers, have them answer the following questions:
- Have you ever been in a similar situation to the one in the picture? If so, what happened?
- What are best things to do for each of the situations pictured? (e.g., use a cellular phone to call for help, wait for the traffic police to come, wait for someone passing to help you)

| 7 | PARTNER | SONG | ⬍ |

Language Focus: Reading and interpreting the meaning of a song in English
Time: 10-15 minutes

ADJUSTING THE LEVEL

Down: Explain that "my baby" is a slang expression for a girlfriend or a boyfriend. Before students do the activity, read the words of the song aloud and discuss the meaning of each stanza in the song.

Up: Have the pairs write a summary of what is happening in the song.

| 8 | PARTNER | SONG | ⬍ |

Language Focus: Describing people
Time: 10 minutes

ADJUSTING THE LEVEL

Down: Before students do the activity, list words and phrases to describe people on the board. Have students identify those that describe the singer, those that describe "my baby," and those that do not describe either.

> EXAMPLE
> attractive, likes to stay in one place, is in love, likes to party, likes to move around, not faithful in love, faithful in love, funny, tall and handsome

Up: After students do the activity, have them work in small groups and tell the story of the song from the point of view of either the singer or "my baby."

> EXAMPLE
> I am young and free. I like to visit new places and see new people. I go all around the United States and Latin America. There is this guy in the States who really likes me. But I am not ready to settle down. I don't want to have a permanent relationship with one person right now.

| 9 | GROUP | SONG | ⬍ |

Language Focus: Writing a song
Time: 15-30 minutes

ADJUSTING THE LEVEL

Down: Model doing the activity with the class. Possible topics are: *my old friend, my new car.*

Up: Have students choose a favorite song in English and write down the lyrics and a summary of what the song is about. This work can be posted for students to share.

PROJECT   APPENDIX 8

The Desert

| 1 | GROUP | RESEARCH | ⬍ |

Language Focus: Using sources to get information, using geographic terms in English
Classroom Tip: Have atlases available in the classroom. You might also have books about deserts written in simple English.
Time: 10 minutes (In addition, students do research outside of class. You may want to allow five to ten minutes of class time to explain the activity.)

ADJUSTING THE LEVEL

Down: To help prepare students for the activity, display a map of the world that shows deserts and other geographical features. Help students to find the key used to identify deserts and to pronounce the desert names in English.

Up: Have groups research the following topics:
  1. How are all deserts alike? How are they different?
  2. Where does water in deserts come from?

| 2 | GROUP | RESEARCH | ⬆ |

Language Focus: Using various sources to get information, using geographic terms in English, describing geographic areas
Time: 20-30 minutes (In addition, students do research outside of class.)

ADJUSTING THE LEVEL

Up: Have students write their findings in two or three paragraphs, in addition to making the picture. For example, they can list types of desert plants and animals and how these plants and animals adapt to survive in the desert.

EPISODE
9
THE MOTEL

THEME Being Polite

| 1 | PARTNER | DISCUSSION | ▲ |

Language Focus: Understanding ways to be polite in English
Time: 10-15 minutes

ADJUSTING THE LEVEL
Up: After students do the activity, have them give reasons for their answers. For example, the woman at the diner isn't polite because she doesn't give an apology (*I am sorry, but we're closed.*) or give reasons (*I am sorry, but we're closed. I need to get home to my family.*)

Then have students work in groups and discuss ways that each of the conversations could be made either more or less polite. Have groups choose one situation and make up a conversation.

> EXAMPLE
> 1. We're closed.
>   *More polite:* I'm sorry. It's closing time. I can't help you.
> 2. Why don't I just sleep in the car?
>   *More polite:* Let me sleep in the car. It's fine with me. I don't want to be any bother to you.

Have groups act out their conversations for the class.

| 2 | PARTNER | WAYS TO SAY IT | ⬍ |

Language Focus: Using polite expressions, making requests
Time: 10 minutes

ADJUSTING THE LEVEL
Down: Write the expressions on the board and have students repeat them. Present situations such as the following and call on individual students to make polite requests, using the expressions on the board.

> SITUATIONS
> have some paper   borrow this CD
> use your dictionary   watch your TV

Up: Have pairs make up a list of things that they might request from each of the following people:
- a teacher
- a landlord
- a roommate

Have pairs play a game with another pair. Each pair states one item from their list. The other pair makes it into a polite request (*Do you mind if I turn on the TV?*) and guesses who probably made the request (*a student,*

a tenant/boarder, or *a roommate*). Each pair gets one point for each correct request and for each correct guess. The pair with the most points wins.

THEME Helping Someone

| 3 | GROUP | BRAINSTORM | ⬍ |

Language Focus: Discussing everyday activities, describing everyday situations
Time: 10-15 minutes

ADJUSTING THE LEVEL
Down: If possible, replay the video and have students look specifically for the ways Alberto helps Rebecca. They should write them down as they watch. Otherwise, have students retell what happens to Rebecca and Alberto in the episode and what the pair does.

Up: Have students do the activity again, this time about one of the following scenarios: how Rebecca helps Kevin, how Rebecca helps Mr. Casey, how Mr. Casey helps Rebecca.

As a follow-up, have groups list ways in which they have helped others during the last week.

| 4 | CLASS | GAME | ▼ |

Language Focus: Offering help for problems
Time: 15-20 minutes

ADJUSTING THE LEVEL
Down: With the class, brainstorm five or six problems (you can use those in the activity). Then brainstorm two or three ways to help a person who has each problem. Write problems and offers for help on the board.

> EXAMPLE
> A: My car broke down.
> B: I can drive you any place you need to go.
> or
> B: I can call my mechanic for you. He's very good at finding problems and he's not very expensive.

THEME Answering Machines

| 5 | GROUP | SURVEY | ▲ |

Language Focus: Giving opinions, interviewing
Classroom Tip: Discuss answering machines with the class. Find out how many students have an answering machine at home or at work, how many have voicemail, and how many have neither.
Time: 10 minutes

ADJUSTING THE LEVEL
Up: As a follow-up, ask the groups to discuss why they gave the answers that they did to questions 2, 3, and 4.

Then have groups list the advantages and disadvantages of answering machines, both for the person with the machine and for the person calling. Have groups share lists.

6 | **PARTNER** | **ROLE-PLAY** ▼

Language Focus: Leaving messages on the phone, using telephone language

Classroom Tip: Review standard phrases one might use on an answering machine or voicemail such as the following: *I can't take your call at this time. Leave your name and number after the tone . . .*
Hi,_____. This is_____. I am calling at 8 o'clock. Please call me back as soon as possible.

Time: 15-20 minutes

ADJUSTING THE LEVEL

Down: For Part A, model writing two or three telephone messages with the class.

For Part B, to structure the activity, tell students to leave messages for one of the following situations:

- You have an extra ticket for a concert tomorrow night. You ask your friend if he/she wants to buy the ticket.
- You think that you left your notebook in your friend's car. Ask about it.
- You are supposed to meet your friend at a restaurant at 7:30. Tell him/her that you will be late and that you will arrive at 8:00.

INFORMATION GAP Dating

7 | **PARTNER** | **INFORMATION GAP** ▲▼

Language Focus: Describing people, describing people's likes and dislikes, asking for and giving information

Time: 15-20 minutes

ADJUSTING THE LEVEL

Down: Before students do the activity, have Student As and Student Bs work in separate groups. The Student A group discusses what it sees in the pictures on page 5. The Student B group discusses what it sees in the pictures on page 6. In their discussion, students should be sure to answer the following question: *What does _____ like to do?*

After pairs do the activity, have them review their matches, using this format: David and Debby should date because they both like music.

Up: Have pairs do a role-play for two of the people they matched. The pair is meeting each other for the first time and they are discussing the things that they like to do. Pairs should try to have at least eight exchanges. Pairs can present their role-plays to the class.

Staying in a Motel

1 | **PARTNER** | **RESEARCH** ▲▼

Language Focus: Describing places, learning about customs/culture, using interview skills

Classroom Tip: Have students use their dictionaries or have dictionaries available. You also want to have available brochures from hotels for students to refer to. Have pairs share answers to Part A as a class.

Time: 10 minutes (In addition, students do fieldwork outside of class. You may want to allow 10-15 minutes of class time to explain the activity.)

ADJUSTING THE LEVEL

Down: Have students do Part A in class, using dictionaries, and have the class share answers.

Before students do Part B, show a brochure for a hotel/motel and go over the language to describe hotel/motel facilities and services. Also, have volunteers discuss the information they want to know before they book a hotel room.

After students do the activity, have them identify services that hotels/motels offer (exercise room, pool, extra space, free breakfast, etc.) and rank them in order of importance.

Up: For Part B, tell pairs to get as much information as they can about the facilities at the hotel/motel they are researching and the services it offers. Have pairs report their information in the form of a paragraph or a brochure that promotes the hotel/motel.

2 | **GROUP** | **COMPARISONS** ▼

Language Focus: Making comparisons

Time: 20 minutes

ADJUSTING THE LEVEL

Down: Write the following sentence frames on the board. Tell students to use structures like these as they work together to answer the questions in the activity.

_____ has more rooms than _____.
_____ is more expensive than _____.
_____ is a better value than _____.
_____ is a better place to stay because _____.

EPISODE
10
NEGOTIATIONS

THEME Good and Bad Dreams

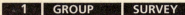

Language Focus: Talking about personal experiences, interviewing
Time: 15 minutes

ADJUSTING THE LEVEL

Up: Have students in their groups each tell about one of the following:
- a good dream he/she has had recently
- a bad dream he/she has had recently
- a dream he/she has often

Have each student report on the most interesting dreams to someone in another group.

2 | TEAM | GAME ▲

Language Focus: Using vocabulary, practicing English spellings
Classroom Tip: You may want students to use their dictionaries or make dictionaries available to students so that they can check words and their spellings.
Time: 10 minutes

ADJUSTING THE LEVEL

Up: As students do the game, have them use each word on their list in a sentence. Teams need to have both correct words and correct sentences: they get one point for each word and one for each sentence. The team with the most points wins.

THEME Bargaining

3 | GROUP | DISCUSSION ⬍

Language Focus: Discussing customs/culture
Time: 15-20 minutes

ADJUSTING THE LEVEL

Down: If possible, replay the part of the video that shows Rebecca bargaining with the mechanic. Ask these questions:
- What does Rebecca give up?
- What does she get?
- What does the mechanic get?

If this is not possible, have students retell what happens in the scene with the mechanic.

Explain that bargaining is not very common in the United States since prices in most stores are fixed, but it is sometimes done, in situations like the following: buying a damaged item in a store, buying a used item from someone, using a taxi that does not have a meter, or taking a taxi a long distance.

Up: Have groups share their answers. Then have groups rank countries from those in which bargaining is very common (all three answers are yes) to those in which bargaining is not very common (all three answers are no).

Finally, have individual students write a paragraph about a time they got a really good bargain or made a really bad bargain. Have them share their paragraphs with their groups.

4 | PARTNER | GAME ▼

Language Focus: Bargaining, using language for buying things, using vocabulary for household items
Time: 10-15 minutes

ADJUSTING THE LEVEL

Down: Model several more dialogues to illustrate the language of bargaining and write them on the board.

> EXAMPLE
> A: How much is this (couch)?
> B: It's $100.
> A: I really don't want to spend more than $70. Is $70 OK?
> B: I'd be giving it away. I want at least $90.
> A: How about $80 in cash? I'll be back with my van in an hour to pick it up. You won't have to move it.
> B: OK. It's a deal.

Point out useful language for (1) asking for prices, (2) offering a price, and (3) making a deal.

THEME Selling Your Car

5 | PARTNER | INTERVIEW ▲

Language Focus: Discussing customs, comparing ways to do something, interviewing
Time: 10-15 minutes

ADJUSTING THE LEVEL

Up: As a follow-up, have pairs try to sell the car in two ways — one in writing and one orally.
- Have them each write an ad for the car.
- Have them make up two role-plays of at least eight exchanges in which each tries to sell the car in the activity to the other for the price he/she wants.

Have pairs share their answers, ads, and role-plays with other pairs.

GAME Car Repairs

6 | GROUP | GAME ⬍

Language Focus: Using vocabulary related to cars
Classroom Tip: You might want to have available in the classroom a picture dictionary that shows a car with the parts labeled (including the inside parts of a car).
Time: 20-30 minutes

ADJUSTING THE LEVEL

Down: Before students do the activity, discuss the function of each of the car parts on page 6 with the class. Refer to the pictures in the book and any available dictionaries in the discussion. Be sure to model the pronunciation of the names of the car parts.

As an additional activity, show an overhead of a car and have students name as many parts as they can. You write labels on the picture as students identify parts.

Up: After the students have played the game, have pairs write the function of six of the parts of the car on page 6. Have pairs read their descriptions to the class. If the class can guess all six parts on the first try, that pair is a winner.

PROJECT   APPENDIX 10

Native Americans

1 | GROUP | RESEARCH ▲

Language Focus: Using various sources to get information, reporting information
Classroom Tip: You may want to have available books about Native Americans written in fairly simple English, such as those intended for children. Illustrated books would be especially useful for this activity.
Time: 20-25 minutes (In addition, students do research outside of class.)

ADJUSTING THE LEVEL

Up: Have students do some additional research for this part of the project. Have each group select one Native American tribe and find out the following information:
  1. Where did the tribe live?
  2. In what kinds of houses did the tribe live?
  3. How did the tribe get food?
  4. What were some things that the tribe produced?
   Also, have pairs of students read a Native American tale. Many of these are available in illustrated versions. Have each pair retell the story to the class. They should also tell a few facts about the tribe that originated the tale or the version of the tale. When all pairs have finished, have students discuss similarities or differences of these tales with traditional stories from their countries.

2 | CLASS | DISCUSSION ▼

Language Focus: Discussing customs/culture
Time: 10-15 minutes

ADJUSTING THE LEVEL

Down: Review information about the dream catcher from the *Connect with English* episode. Explain how the dream catcher worked: good dreams went through the hole in the center and bad dreams were caught and stopped by strings.
   To help the discussion, ask students questions like these:
• Do people talk about their dreams in their culture/ country?
• Are there beliefs about ways to have good dreams or to avoid bad dreams?
• Do people believe that what they remember from dreams will come true?

EPISODE

11

PHOTOS AND FAREWELLS

THEME Taking Photos

| 1 | GROUP | DISCUSSION | ▲ |

Language Focus: Giving advice, talking about places
Time: 15 minutes

ADJUSTING THE LEVEL

Up: Have students ask these additional questions and record the results on a separate piece of paper:
  • Why will the pictures of the place be interesting?
  • Is it best to take long shots or closeups of the place?
  • Why are the people there interesting?
  If possible, have volunteers bring in pictures they have taken of the local area and tell what the pictures show and why they decided to take pictures of the place. If many students have pictures available, you might arrange a contest in which students try to identify the places and then have the class vote for the most interesting photograph (with each student giving the reasons for his/her choice).

| 2 | PARTNER | WAYS TO SAY IT | ↕ |

Language Focus: Using polite expressions, making requests
Time: 10 minutes

ADJUSTING THE LEVEL

Down: Write the complete expressions from the activity on the board, underlining the part to repeat. Then erase the board. Present a situation, such as: *take a picture of your baby.* Students work in pairs and list as many complete expressions as they can in two minutes that relate to the situation (e.g., *May I take a picture of your beautiful baby?, Could I take a picture of your baby?*).

Up: Review expressions for granting or refusing permission.
  EXAMPLE
  Granting permission:
  You can (take pictures here).

  Refusing permission:
  You can't (take pictures here).
  You are not allowed to (take pictures here).
  It is forbidden to (take pictures here).
  I would really rather that you didn't.

Encourage students to work in pairs to use these expressions and make up role-plays for the following situations:
  • A person in a museum wants to take a picture, but you know that pictures are not allowed.

  • A person on the street asks to take your picture. You are on your way to a soccer match and you are dressed up in the colors of your team.

THEME Taking a Bus Trip

| 3 | PARTNER | INTERVIEW | ▲ |

Language Focus: Talking about past activities, talking about personal experiences, interviewing
Time: 10-15 minutes

ADJUSTING THE LEVEL

Up: Have pairs continue the interview with the following questions:
  • Think of a bus trip you have made. Where did you go?
  • How long did the trip take?
  • What did you see on the trip?
  • What did you do on the trip?
  • Do you like to travel by bus? Why or why not?
Each student writes a paragraph about his/her partner's bus trip. Pairs then share paragraphs.

| 4 | PARTNER | ROLE-PLAY | ↕ |

Language Focus: Asking for and giving information about schedules
Classroom Tip: You may want to have actual bus schedules available for students to read or to use in follow-up activities.
Time: 15 minutes

ADJUSTING THE LEVEL

Down: Model the activity by writing a sample conversation like the following on the board. First, you should play the customer and have a volunteer play the clerk. Then, have student volunteers play both roles.
  EXAMPLE
  A: I'd like a one-way trip to _____.
  B: What time would you like to leave?
  A: In the morning.
  B: There's a bus at _____. That'll be $_____ .

Up: To extend the activity, provide students with actual bus schedules or show the schedules on an overhead. Have students prepare a role-play like those in the activity. In the role-play, they can also ask for arrival times of the buses. The "clerk" can ask if the "customer" wants to pay by cash, check, or credit card.

THEME Speeding

| 5 | GROUP | SURVEY | ↕ |

Language Focus: Discussing customs, making comparisons, giving opinions, interviewing
Classroom Tip: Present the following formulas so that students can make comparisons between miles and kilometers:
  1 kilometer = .621 miles
  1 mile = 1.609 kilometers
Time: 15-20 minutes

ADJUSTING THE LEVEL

Down: Before students do Part C, write the following on the board to guide them in their summary of results:

- Most people think that the speed limit in their country is (too high, too low, just right).
- More women than men think that the speed limit in their country is (too high, too low, just right).
- More men than women think that the speed limit in their country is (too high, too low, just right).
- Most women think that the speed limit in their country is (too high, too low, just right).
- Most men think that the speed limit in their country is (too high, too low, just right).

Up: Have each group write a report on its findings. The speed limits can be made in the form of a chart, from highest to lowest speeds. The findings to question 1 can be made in the form of a pie chart, and the findings to question 2 in the form of a bar graph (with bars for men and women for each choice — too low, too high, just right). Provide copies of each group's results to the other groups so that each group can make a summary of class results.

| 6 | PARTNER | ROLE-PLAY | ▼ |

Language Focus: Persuading someone not to do something, making excuses
Time: 20 minutes

ADJUSTING THE LEVEL

Down: Model the activity for the students. Choose one situation, and with the class compose a dialogue for it. Write the dialogue on the board.

    EXAMPLE
    Situation 4
    A: Officer, here's my license. Was I going too fast?
    B: I'm afraid so. The speed radar showed you were going 15 miles above the speed limit.
    A: I'm sorry. I didn't realize it. You see my speedometer's broken. I thought I was going the same speed as the other cars.
    B: 15 miles over the speed limit is quite a lot.
    (and so on)

INFORMATION GAP
Immigrants in the U.S.

| 7 | PARTNER | INFORMATION GAP | ▲ |

Language Focus: Asking for and giving information, describing people's background
Time: 10-15 minutes

ADJUSTING THE LEVEL

Up: Have pairs do research and find four interesting facts about one of the people. They can use encyclopedias or the Internet. Have pairs share the information they find about the person with the class. Have the class discuss what they know about the person and his or her accomplishments. Have them vote on the person that they would most like to meet.

P R O J E C T   APPENDIX 11

Nature and Natural Beauty

| 1 | GROUP | RESEARCH | |

Language Focus: Describing places, reporting information, persuading others
Classroom Tip: Have travel brochures or travel books for places of natural beauty available for students to refer to.
Time: 20-30 minutes (In addition, students do research outside of class.)

ADJUSTING THE LEVEL

Down: Give information from travel books and brochures about a site of natural beauty such as the redwood forest in California, the Everglades in Florida, or volcanoes in Hawaii. If possible, put some of the information on overheads. Have students read the material. Guide the class in completing a chart for the place like the ones in the activity.

Before students give their presentations to the class, have them present them to another group. That group asks questions for clarification and provides suggestions for revision.

E P I S O D E

12

A NEW HOME

THEME Living in a Boarding House

1 | PARTNER | INTERVIEW | ▲

Language Focus: Discussing likes and dislikes, interviewing
Time: 10-15 minutes

ADJUSTING THE LEVEL
Up: After pairs do the activity, have them list the advantages and disadvantages of living in a boarding house.

> EXAMPLE
> *Advantages*
> •low rent
> •having people around to talk to
>
> *Disadvantages*
> •trying to be quiet all the time
> •not being able to invite friends to listen to music
> •not being able to watch a TV program I want

Then have pairs rank each list — from most important advantage to least important advantage, and from most important disadvantage to least important disadvantage. Have students share their lists with another pair.

Finally, have each student write a paragraph about why he/she would or would not like to live in a boarding house. Have students share paragraphs in small groups.

2 | GROUP | DISCUSSION | ▲

Language Focus: Discussing rules, negotiating
Time: 15 minutes

ADJUSTING THE LEVEL
Up: After students do the activity, have them do it again, this time deciding on eight rules from the list.

Have groups compare their lists of rules. Have individual students tell what rule on the list would be the most difficult for them to live with.

THEME Cultural Differences

3 | GROUP | COMPARISONS | ▼

Language Focus: Discussing customs/culture, interviewing
Time: 15-20 minutes

ADJUSTING THE LEVEL
Down: Before students do the activity, go over the items in the list. Explain that the items in the list are not unusual in the culture of the United States and Canada. Talk about

your personal experience or experiences of people you know in relation to the items.

Then have the class discuss any differences from their countries. Have students answer the question: *Which of the items would be unusual in your country?* With the class, discuss why the differences occur.

4 | PARTNER | WAYS TO SAY IT | ↕

Language Focus: Asking for permission, making requests
Classroom Tip: Have students discuss any differences they have noticed between the way in which people from different countries make polite requests.
Time: 10-15 minutes

ADJUSTING THE LEVEL
Down: Before students do the activity, go over the expressions in the box. With the class, brainstorm a list of requests that people living in a boarding house might make of one another and of the person who runs the boarding house. Then write each request on a separate piece of paper. Have students take turns choosing a paper and requesting the item on the paper.

Up: Have pairs role-play a dialogue. One is Nancy and the other is a visitor to the house. The visitor is a friend of Angela's who is waiting for Angela to return. In the role-play, Angela's friend makes at least three requests. Have pairs present their role-plays to the class. Review expressions for declining requests, such as *I'm sorry. I'd rather that you didn't _____*, as well as expressions for granting requests such as *OK., Fine., No problem., Go ahead.*

THEME Growing Old

5 | PARTNER | SHARING | ↕

Language Focus: Asking for and giving information, describing people, interviewing
Time: 20-30 minutes

ADJUSTING THE LEVEL
Down: Model the activity by having students ask you the questions. Write the answers on the board, and with the class compose a paragraph about the person you know.

Then brainstorm words to describe the personal qualities of people (students can use them for question 8). You might want to have students describe the people in the video:

> Rebecca: dedicated, talented, helpful, generous, fun to be with, friendly
> Melaku: hardworking, formal, friendly, smart

Up: Have students each write a paragraph about the person they have chosen. Have students share their paragraphs in small groups.

| 6 | PARTNER | INFORMATION GAP | ▲ |

Language Focus: Asking for and giving information, discussing budgets
Time: 15 minutes

ADJUSTING THE LEVEL
Up: Have students make pie charts of percentages showing how Rebecca and Nancy spend their money.

Have students make a pie chart showing a good budget for Rebecca or Nancy, or a good budget for a single person or for a family of four. Have them first make a list of items to include in the budget such as rent/mortgage, food, clothing, utilities, transportation, entertainment. Point out that in the United States, it is typical for people to spend about 25% of their income on housing and 10-15% on food.

Retirement Homes

| 1 | GROUP | DISCUSSION | ▼ |

Language Focus: Asking for and giving information, giving opinions, discussing customs/culture, using interview skills
Classroom Tip: If possible, have someone who works in a retirement house talk about his/her work and the kinds of services that the retirement home offers to older people.
Time: 15 minutes

ADJUSTING THE LEVEL
Down: To model the activity, have students ask you the questions. Then have them tell any information you gave that was surprising to them.

If possible, discuss the kinds of care available in the United States: home care, nursing home care, retirement homes where people have individual apartments, and so on.

| 2 | GROUP | SURVEY | ↕ |

Language Focus: Giving opinions, using interview skills
Time: 10-15 minutes (In addition, students do fieldwork outside of class.)

ADJUSTING THE LEVEL
Down: Have students first do the activity by interviewing another member of their group. After students do the fieldwork, have the groups get together to tally their answers and discuss results.

Up: Have students discuss treatment of older people in their countries/cultures. Have them answer these questions:
- Do retirement homes exist?
- Do most people go to retirement homes?
- What happens when old people can no longer care for themselves?
- When do people go to retirement homes?
- Who pays for the cost of the retirement home?

Have students do additional fieldwork and find out about two or three local retirement homes and the kinds of services they provide. They can do this by interviewing members of the community or calling up the homes. Have students report their findings to the class.

EPISODE
13
JOB HUNTING

THEME Giving Directions

| 1 | PARTNER | WAYS TO SAY IT | ↕ |

Language Focus: Giving directions
Time: 15-20 minutes

ADJUSTING THE LEVEL
Down: Before students do the activity, have them locate various places on the map and discuss what people can do or obtain in each. Then model giving directions for one or two places and have students follow along. (You might also model how to get to local places from school.)

> EXAMPLE
> S: How do I get to Cool Mo's Bakery?
> T: Go straight on Central Avenue for three blocks. When you get to University Avenue, turn left.

Have students identify the direction words you use, and list them on the board.

Up: Have students do additional role-plays in pairs. One pretends to be a tourist in need of something — for example, a place to stay, a pharmacy, a restaurant. The other gives the name of an appropriate place and directions to it.

| 2 | GROUP | GAME | ↕ |

Language Focus: Giving directions
Time: 15 minutes

ADJUSTING THE LEVEL
Down: Model the activity with the class by giving directions and having students trace the route and identify the building.

Up: Tell students to start from various locations on the map; for example, Broadway Boutique. They need to tell the place they are starting from as they play the game.

THEME International Food

| 3 | PARTNER | INTERVIEW | ▲ |

Language Focus: Using food vocabulary, expressing preferences
Time: 10-15 minutes

ADJUSTING THE LEVEL
Up: With the class, brainstorm a list of dishes in each food category, including the ones pictured.

Have pairs expand the survey by asking two more questions:
- For your favorite kind of food, which dish is your favorite?
- What other dishes have you tried?

Have pairs report the results to class. Have the class determine the favorite kinds of foods and favorite dishes in the food categories.

| 4 | PARTNER | SHARE | ↓ |

Language Focus: Using food vocabulary, expressing preferences
Classroom Tip: Have pictures of food available; these can be found in picture dictionaries, supermarket fliers, or newspapers.
Time: 15 minutes

ADJUSTING THE LEVEL
Down: Model the activity by telling students about your favorite meal. Then have volunteers tell about favorite meals from their country. As students do the activity, display pictures of food, as suggested above, so that students can find the vocabulary needed to describe foods and ingredients.

THEME Using Computers

| 5 | PARTNER | CATEGORIES | ▼ |

Language Focus: Using vocabulary for occupations, using vocabulary related to computers
Time: 15-20 minutes

ADJUSTING THE LEVEL
Down: Before students do the activity, work with the class to complete charts like the following for a few of the jobs. Write the charts on the board.

ARCHITECT

What the person does:	makes designs of buildings
Where the person works:	office, at building sites
How computers can help:	in drawing designs, in testing that buildings are safe

| 6 | GROUP | DISCUSSION | ▲ |

Language Focus: Using vocabulary related to computers, expressing personal opinions
Time: 15-20 minutes

ADJUSTING THE LEVEL
Up: Have each group write a report of results of the survey and the discussion. Have the groups share their reports with the class.

Then have students work in pairs and write a paragraph about how students in the class use computers, such as the following: *Most students in my class use computers. Most use them at work. About one-quarter of the students use them for entertainment.*

Finally, have students work on their own and write a paragraph on one of the following topics:
- Why I like/don't like to use computers
- How I use computers

INFORMATION GAP
Reading Bulletin Boards

7	PARTNER	INFORMATION GAP	⬍

Language Focus: Using vocabulary related to jobs, reading want ads
Time: 15-20 minutes

ADJUSTING THE LEVEL
Down: Before students do the activity, show them several simple job ads. Use an overhead transparency, or write the ads on the board. With the class, complete charts in the following format, which matches that in the activity:

Position/Job:
Hours:
Contact:
Requirements:

Up: Give students actual pages of want ads from newspapers or other sources available to you. Have students try to find jobs that Rebecca might apply for. Have them write the information in the chart format shown above.

8	PARTNER	DISCUSSION	⬍

Language Focus: Using vocabulary related to jobs, supporting opinions
Time: 10-25 minutes

ADJUSTING THE LEVEL
Down: Before students do the activity, write the following questions on the board:

1. Does the job match Rebecca's skills?
2. Are the hours good for Rebecca?
3. Does the job match Rebecca's interests?

Model how to answer them for one of the jobs in Activity 7. Tell students to use the questions as they work on the activity. This will help them to justify their answers.

EXAMPLE
Female Singer
The job is good for Rebecca because it matches her skills and interests. The hours are good for her because she can work during the evenings.

Up: Have the pairs choose one of the jobs that they think is good for Rebecca. Have them role-play a job interview. One student plays Rebecca; the other student plays the "contact" person. Tell students to make sure that "Rebecca" tells why she is good for the job. Pairs can present their role-play to the class.

PROJECT APPENDIX 1

Culture Shock

1	PARTNER	RESEARCH	⬍

Language Focus: Describing places, using sources to get information
Classroom Tip: Have available resources that students can use for reference, such as travel guidebooks and brochures.
Time: 10 minutes (In addition, students do research outside of class. You may want to allow class time for pairs to complete their charts.)

ADJUSTING THE LEVEL
Down: Lead a discussion in which you and students tell of personal experiences with culture shock in travels to new places.

Then, with the class, model how to do the activity. Have students use information from the video to fill in the categories in the chart in Activity 1. Have students tell what things in the video were new to them or different in their countries. Write the answers on the board. (Keep the answers for Activity 2.)

Finally, present some materials that students can use in their research, such as guidebooks and brochures. Help students find materials by describing sources available in your local area.

Up: Tell students to write a paragraph about each of the topics in the chart.

2	GROUP	DISCUSSION	⬇

Language Focus: Describing places, expressing opinions
Time: 15 minutes

ADJUSTING THE LEVEL
Down: Model how to do the activity. As a class, have students use the material from the video as the basis for answering the questions. They can use the information gathered in Activity 1.

EPISODE
14

A BAD DAY

THEME
Sharing Experiences with a Friend

| 1 | TEAM | GAME | ▲ |

Language Focus: Talking about everyday activities and experiences, using the past tense
Time: 5 minutes

ADJUSTING THE LEVEL
Up: After students do the activity, have them work in pairs and role-play an actual three-minute telephone conversation between Rebecca and Sandy. Rebecca and Sandy tell what has happened to them since Rebecca left Boston.

| 2 | PARTNER | INTERVIEW | ⬍ |

Language Focus: Talking about oneself, interviewing
Time: 10 minutes

ADJUSTING THE LEVEL
Down: Before students do the activity, have them ask you the questions in the interview as a class. Explain your answers so that students can get an understanding of the questions.

Up: Have pairs do a follow-up survey. They should copy the chart on a separate piece of paper but write this question at the top: *Who is it good to tell about . . .?* Pairs should get together in groups to compare answers. Encourage students to defend their answers by telling why it is good or not good to tell certain people.

THEME Having a Bad Day

| 3 | PARTNER | WAYS TO SAY IT | ⬍ |

Language Focus: Expressing sympathy and understanding
Time: 10-15 minutes

ADJUSTING THE LEVEL
Down: Before students do the activity, write the expressions of sympathy/empathy on the board. Orally present several pieces of bad news (e.g., *I lost my wallet. My mother is ill. I didn't get the job I wanted.*). Have students respond orally, first in groups and then individually, using the expressions on the board.

Up: With the class, go over the situations in Activity 3 and model a follow-up question (e.g., *What are you doing to find your dog? Have you started to look for a new job?*)

Then have students work in pairs and choose a piece of bad news (e.g., *My car broke down.*) They make up a role-play of at least six exchanges in which one student tells the bad news to the other, who responds and asks follow-up questions. Pairs can present their role-plays to the class.

| 4 | PARTNER | INTERVIEW | ▲ |

Language Focus: Talking about personal experiences and activities
Time: 10 minutes

ADJUSTING THE LEVEL
Up: Have students write a paragraph about a bad day they had and what they did to feel better. Present the following questions for them to answer in their paragraph:
• What happened to you on the bad day?
• How did you feel?
• What did you do to feel better?
• When did you begin to feel better?
• How did you feel the next day?
• Was the problem ever solved?
Have students share their paragraphs in small groups.

THEME Making a Date

| 5 | PARTNER | ROLE-PLAY | ▼ |

Language Focus: Asking someone out on a date (inviting), accepting or rejecting an offer for a date (an invitation), ending a conversation
Time: 10-15 minutes

ADJUSTING THE LEVEL
Down: With the class, write out one or two dialogues for accepting or rejecting a date. Students can use the language in the book or their own ideas.
    EXAMPLES
    A: Hi, I'd like to speak to ____. This is ____.
    B: This is _____.
    A: There's a jazz concert in the park next Sunday afternoon. It's free. Would you like to come with me?
    B: Oh, I really like jazz. I'd love to go.
    A: Good. I'll call you on Saturday to make plans.
    B: OK. I'll be looking forward to the concert.

    A: Hi, this is ___. Is _____ there?
    B: This is _____.
    A: Would you like to go to the beach with me on Saturday?
    B: Oh, I'd like to go, but I already have plans. I'm going out of town with my family.
    A: OK. Maybe we can do something next weekend.
    B: OK. Fine.
    A: I hope you have a good trip this weekend. Bye.

In the dialogues on the board, have students point out ways to begin and end conversations on the phone, as well as ways to invite and accept or reject invitations.

Language Focus: Giving opinions, making generalizations
Time: 15 minutes

ADJUSTING THE LEVEL
Down: Have groups report their results to the class. Write the following sentence frames on the board for students to use in their reports:

All people in the group agree with sentence ____.
Most people in the group agree with sentence ____.
All people in the group disagree with sentence ____.
Most people in the group disagree with sentence ____.

Each group should have one sentence for each item. Ask the groups to report their results. Have volunteers with varying opinions tell their ideas, and have volunteers tell what is commonly done in their countries.

GAME **The Job Interview**

7 | **GROUP** | **GAME** ⬍

Language Focus: Writing sentences relating to job interviews, using the language of the work place
Time: 20 minutes (The game can be played several times throughout the course of the episode.)

ADJUSTING THE LEVEL
Down: Go over the examples of game cards and topics in the book. Then with the class, brainstorm more items. Encourage students to think about things that they have read and their personal experiences in job interviews. Write ideas on the board.

Up: After students play the game, have groups each come up with a list of top ten "dos and don'ts" for people on a job interview. Have groups present their lists to the class. The class votes on the best list.

PROJECT APPENDIX 2

Looking for a Job

1 | **PARTNER** | **RESEARCH** ▲

Language Focus: Using vocabulary for occupations, reading want ads
Classroom Tip: You may want to provide help-wanted ads from newspapers or other sources for students to work with.
Time: 15 minutes

ADJUSTING THE LEVEL
Up: Before students do the task, have them discuss how they will look for the jobs (e.g., alphabetically by category under certain headings). After they do the task, find out which pair found the most jobs. Have them explain where they found the listings.
   Next, ask students to answer the following questions in groups:
• Which job on the list would you most like to have? Why?
• Which job on the list would you least like to have? Why?
• What was the most unusual job you found in the want ads?

2 | **GROUP** | **INTERVIEW** ▼

Language Focus: Interviewing, discussing jobs, making generalizations
Time: 5-10 minutes (In addition, students do fieldwork outside of class.)

ADJUSTING THE LEVEL
Down: Before students do the interview with people outside of class, have them ask you and other class members the question: *How did you find your job?* As a class, discuss which column should be checked for each answer. Write the results on the board. Keep the results so that students can compare them with the results from their interviews.

E P I S O D E
15
A NIGHT OUT

THEME Giving Compliments

| 1 | GROUP | ROLE-PLAY | ▼ |

Language Focus: Giving compliments
Time: 10-15 minutes

ADJUSTING THE LEVEL

Down: Before students do the activity, present/review common language forms for giving compliments by writing phrases like the following on the board:
- I love/I like (your haircut).
- That's a great/good/wonderful (jacket).
- Those are great/good/wonderful (jeans).
- You're a great/good/wonderful (writer).
- You're great at (explaining things).

Have students take turns orally giving compliments to you and to other class members.

| 2 | GROUP | DISCUSSION | ◆ |

Language Focus: Giving opinions
Time: 10-15 minutes

ADJUSTING THE LEVEL

Down: Before students do the activity in groups, prompt discussion by asking the class these questions:
- To whom do you usually give compliments?
- Is it always OK to give compliments to someone you know well?
- Is it always OK to give a compliment to someone you don't know well?
- Do you give compliments to your boss or your teacher? If so, when?
- Is it OK to give compliments to people like your boss?

Up: As students do the activity, have each group list three situations when it is not appropriate to give a compliment and write why. Have groups share their lists with the class.
   Then have students discuss these statements as a class:
- It is always appropriate to give a compliment.
- Sometimes a compliment can be mistaken for an insult.

| 3 | PARTNER | INTERVIEW | ▼ |

Language Focus: Asking for and giving information, giving personal information
Classroom Tip: After partners complete the interview, have pairs exchange information.
Time: 15 minutes

ADJUSTING THE LEVEL

Down: Before students do the activity, have the class ask you the questions. Have volunteers write the answers on the board. If necessary, repeat the activity with several other volunteers answering.

THEME A First Date

| 4 | GROUP | DISCUSSION | ▲ |

Language Focus: Talking about everyday activities, talking about customs
Time: 10-15 minutes

ADJUSTING THE LEVEL

Up: Have students as a class discuss any differences in what is commonly done on first dates in their countries.
   Have students write a paragraph about one of the following topics:
- My "Best" First Date
- My "Worst" First Date
- An "Ideal" First Date

Have students share paragraphs in small groups.

| 5 | GROUP | DEBATE | ◆ |

Language Focus: Giving opinions
Time: 20 minutes

ADJUSTING THE LEVEL

Down: Before students do the activity, discuss these questions as a class:
- Is it usual for a couple on their first date to meet one of the person's parents?
- When does this occur?
- When doesn't this occur?
- What does it tell about the relationship between the couple?

Discuss any differences in answers. Explain that in the United States when people introduce their boyfriends/girlfriends to their parents, this often indicates the relationship is serious.

   As students do the activity in groups, help them come up with ideas like the following:

Opinion 1: Alberto knew that his family would not think that he was serious about Rebecca.
Opinion 2: It is not good to surprise someone on a first date. The other person might not like it.

Up: After students do the activity, have each student prepare a one-minute role-play/monologue from one of these viewpoints:
- You are Rebecca: You tell why you didn't mind Alberto taking you to see his parents.
- You are Rebecca: You tell why you were not pleased that Alberto took you to see his parents as a surprise.
- You are Alberto: You tell why you thought it was OK to take Rebecca to see your parents.

Students can present role-plays in small groups.

THEME Making Suggestions

6 PARTNER WAYS TO SAY IT ⇕

Language Focus: Making suggestions
Time: 10-15 minutes

ADJUSTING THE LEVEL

Down: Before students do the activity, ask the class to brainstorm a list of possible solutions to each problem in the activity.

> EXAMPLE
> *Problem:* My math class is difficult.
>
> *Solutions:*
> • You could ask the teacher for help.
> • Why don't you study with friends?
> • I recommend you study math every day.
> • You might get another math book and study it.

Up: Have students work in pairs and choose a problem such as the following: *I don't know where to take someone I just met on our first date.* They make up a role-play of at least six exchanges in which one student tells the problem and the other student gives advice. Tell the student with the problem to reject the first piece of advice and say why. Students can present role-plays to the class.

7 GROUP SHARE ▲

Language Focus: Writing/talking about personal experiences, giving reasons
Time: 15-20 minutes

ADJUSTING THE LEVEL

Up: As a follow-up, have students write a paragraph on the following topic:

> The Best/Worst Advice I Have Ever Received

Have them answer these questions:
• What problem did you have?
• What was the advice? Who gave you the advice?
• Did you follow the advice? What happened?

SONG Go to Sleep

8 PARTNER SONG ▼

Language Focus: Understanding figurative language, reading song lyrics
Time: 10-15 minutes

ADJUSTING THE LEVEL

Down: Before students do the activity in the book, discuss the following underlined items from the song: *The moon is on the rise, barely know, light that's shining.*

Then ask students to draw a picture to illustrate what the song means to them. Have them explain their drawings to their partners.

9 PARTNER SONG ⇕

Language Focus: Retelling information
Classroom Tip: A day or two before students do the activity in class, ask them to think of a song, story, or phrase they learned from their family to use for a class activity.
Time: 20 minutes

ADJUSTING THE LEVEL

Down: Model the activity by presenting a song, story, or phrase from your family and telling what it means to you. Ask students to write three things about what you tell them. Students share what they wrote in small groups.

Up: Have students tell another pair what they learned from their partner.

PROJECT   APPENDIX 3

Tourist Attractions

1 GROUP RESEARCH ⇕

Language Focus: Describing places, using language related to tourism, using reference sources to get information
Classroom Tip: Have sources of information about your local area available, such as guidebooks or brochures from tourist offices.
Time: 10 minutes (In addition, students do research and fieldwork outside of class. You might want to schedule some class time so that groups can prepare their schedules.)

ADJUSTING THE LEVEL

Down: Before students do the activity, brainstorm a list of possible places in your area for tourists to visit and write them on the board. Also, discuss sources of information on these places, such as tourist offices or guidebooks.

Up: Have students write up the information in the form of a brochure with a schedule for a tour. To do this, they need to tell why it is fun or interesting to visit each place.

2 CLASS DISCUSSION ▲

Language Focus: Describing places, negotiating, writing a letter
Time: 20-30 minutes

ADJUSTING THE LEVEL

Up: Have students prepare several schedules for different types of tour groups: parents with children, senior citizens, people interested in nature, people interested in art.

E P I S O D E
16
FIRST DAY OF CLASS

THEME Studying with Friends

| 1 | CLASS | GAME | ▲ |

Language Focus: Talking about school and study habits
Time: 10 minutes

ADJUSTING THE LEVEL

Up: After students complete the game, ask them to find five of the people whose names are on their list. Students should ask these people more questions about their study habits. For example, a student can talk to the person who has his/her name next to the question, *Do you listen to music while you study?* The student might ask, *What kind of music do you listen to?* or *Why do you listen to music while you study?*

Then have the groups make a list of ten good study tips. Have groups share their lists.

| 2 | PARTNER | DISCUSSION | ▼ |

Language Focus: Giving opinions
Classroom Tip: Make sure students understand all of the items on the list.
Time: 10-15 minutes

ADJUSTING THE LEVEL

Down: Model the activity. With the class, go over two or three of the items on the list in the activity and come up with advantages and disadvantages for each.

EXAMPLE
Studying in the library
Good: It is quiet. You can concentrate more easily.
Bad: It takes time to get to the library. The chairs are not comfortable.

THEME The First Day of Class

| 3 | CLASS | BRAINSTORM | ▼ |

Language Focus: Discussing everyday activities, using vocabulary related to school
Time: 10-15 minutes

ADJUSTING THE LEVEL

Down: Before students do the activity in the book, have them name things that they did the first day of this class and list them on the board.

When students begin the activity, tell them to change the items in the list to the present tense. These items will be the start of the list that they are to brainstorm. (Keep the list on the board for use in the next activity.)

| 4 | PARTNER | INTERVIEW | ⇕ |

Language Focus: Talking about past activities, using vocabulary related to school, writing a paragraph
Time: 20-30 minutes

ADJUSTING THE LEVEL

Down: Before students do the activity, model it. Have students ask you the questions and have volunteers write your answers on the board. Then with the class, put together a paragraph using the information on the board. You might want to start with a sentence that tells why you remember that particular first day.

Encourage students to refer to the paragraph on the board and the list from Activity 3 for help with spelling and use of past tense as they write their paragraphs.

Up: Encourage students to ask additional questions and incorporate the answers into the paragraph if appropriate.
EXAMPLE
• Why do you remember that day?
• What happened to you during the time you took the class?
• Was the class a good experience for you?
• What did you learn from that first day?
• What did you learn from the class?

THEME
Not Understanding the Teacher

| 5 | PARTNER | WAYS TO SAY IT | ⇕ |

Language Focus: Indicating you don't understand, asking for help in understanding
Classroom Tip: Explain that "I don't get it." is informal and usually is not appropriate to use in a formal classroom setting.
Time: 10-15 minutes

ADJUSTING THE LEVEL

Down: Go over the expressions in the box, having students repeat them. Then start to give an explanation about some classroom situation, but then speak softly, then too fast, then use a lot of high-level words, and so on. Tell students to communicate to you in words when they don't understand.

Up: This time ask student volunteers to stand up and say something in class (e.g., *The homework for tonight is to* read chapters two and three. or *My phone number is 541-6320.*). Other students respond with an expression from the box, such as *I beg your pardon?*

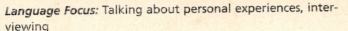

Language Focus: Talking about personal experiences, interviewing
Time: 10-15 minutes

ADJUSTING THE LEVEL

Up: After students do the activity, have them work in small groups and classify each item in the survey as a good or a bad thing to do. They should list reasons and share their lists.

    Then have students work in small groups and write a paragraph of general advice for someone in class who is having trouble understanding the teacher. Have groups share their paragraphs with the class.

GAME **Making New Friends**

| 7 | TEAM | GAME | ◆ |

Language Focus: Writing about personal experiences, interests, and abilities
Time: 30-40 minutes (This game can extend over two or three class periods.)

ADJUSTING THE LEVEL

Down: Model giving information about yourself for each of the topics on the list. Then call on students, give the name of a category, and tell students to give a fact about themselves related to the category. The other class members should write down the most interesting facts they hear. Then students work in pairs and share what they have written.

Up: After students have played the game, have them work in groups of five. Each group writes an article for a school newspaper about the class members. The article should focus on interesting or unusual things about students in the class. The groups can post their articles in the classroom.

Working with Children

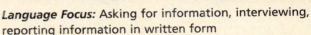

Language Focus: Using various sources to get information
Time: 5-10 minutes (In addition, students do research outside of class.)

ADJUSTING THE LEVEL

Down: Provide students with tips on where to find information (e.g., under "child care" in the Yellow Pages).

Up: Tell students to try all three sources listed in the activity if possible — the telephone book, a newspaper, and the Internet. Have students answer the following questions:
- Which source gave the most information?
- From which source did you get the least information?
- Which source was the easiest to use?

| 2 | PARTNER | RESEARCH | ◆ |

Language Focus: Asking for information, interviewing, reporting information in written form
Time: 20-30 minutes (In addition, students do fieldwork outside of class.)

ADJUSTING THE LEVEL

Down: Before students do the activity, invite someone from a children's program to come to class and have students ask them the questions. This gives students practice both in asking questions and in understanding vocabulary.

    You can have the pairs present their report to you before they give it to the class. Make suggestions and ask questions to help pairs improve their reports.

Up: Have pairs do the activity for two programs. They then make a chart comparing the two programs on the basis of the answers to the questions in the activity. In their reports, students can discuss the advantages and disadvantages of each program.

EPISODE

17

CASEY AT THE BAT

THEME
Sending and Receiving Flowers

1	PARTNER	DISCUSSION	⬍

Language Focus: Talking about culture/customs, talking about important personal events, using vocabulary related to flowers

Classroom Tip: Have available a picture dictionary with pictures of flowers so that students can associate types of flowers with their English names.

Time: 10 minutes

ADJUSTING THE LEVEL

Down: Before students do the activity, discuss the following questions as a class and write the events mentioned on the board:
- When have you received flowers from someone? Was it for a special event?
- When have you given flowers to someone? Was it for a special event?
- What kinds of flowers do people in your country send for special events?

Up: Have students write a paragraph about when flowers are commonly sent in their countries or about one special event when flowers are sent. Have students share paragraphs in small groups.

2	PARTNER	OPINIONS	▼

Language Focus: Giving opinions, discussing customs/culture
Time: 5-10 minutes

ADJUSTING THE LEVEL

Down: Model the activity. Write the sentences in the survey on the board and give your opinions. Also explain U.S. customs.
- Many people in the United States buy flowers once a week. Also, many people have flower gardens.
- In the United States, it is common for both men and women to send flowers to relatives. It is more common for women to receive flowers than men.
- In the United States, many people buy flowers for themselves and use them to decorate their houses.
- A gift of flowers from a man to a woman usually shows that the man likes the woman and is interested in a relationship with her.

THEME Filling Out Forms

3	GROUP	SURVEY	▲

Language Focus: Interviewing, discussing kinds of basic personal information
Time: 10 minutes

ADJUSTING THE LEVEL

Up: After students do the survey, have them work in their groups and write their answers to the following questions:
- What kind of form(s) has everyone filled out?
- What kind of form(s) has no one filled out?
- What kind of form is the easiest to fill out?
- What kind of form is the hardest to fill out?
- How often do people in the group fill out forms?
- Do people in the group like to fill out forms?
Have each group share results with another.

4	CLASS	BRAINSTORM	▲

Language Focus: Using vocabulary related to forms, using vocabulary related to personal information
Classroom Tip: Have available examples of the forms in Activity 3 so that the class can check how close their guesses are. Have students fill out an actual form.
Time: 10-15 minutes

ADJUSTING THE LEVEL

Up: As students do the activity, have them explain why they think the kinds of information are asked for on each form.

As a follow-up, supply students with different types of forms to fill out or ask the class to bring in forms. Have students work in pairs. Each student fills out a form for his/her partner, asking the partner questions and writing the information in the appropriate places.

THEME Casey at the Bat

5	GROUP	STORY	▼

Language Focus: Sequencing events
Classroom Tip: Have available a copy of the poem *Casey at the Bat.* It was written by Ernest Thayer.
Time: 10 minutes
Answer Key: There are no correct or incorrect answers for this activity, as there are several ways to logically sequence these items. To check the sequencing against the action in the poem, supply the students with a copy of *Casey at the Bat* as suggested below.

ADJUSTING THE LEVEL

Down: Before students do the activity, give the following summary or get a copy of the poem *Casey at the Bat* and read it to class; begin with "There was ease in Casey's manner. . ." Make sure that students understand basic facts about baseball: A pitcher throws to the batter. If a batter tries to hit the ball and misses, it's a strike. When a ball is thrown in a certain area, it is also a strike. An umpire judges if a pitch is a strike. After three strikes, a batter loses his/her turn.

Summary: Casey's team is losing 4-2. Casey is the last batter. If he hits a home run, his team wins. If he doesn't get a hit, his team loses. Casey comes up to bat. He isn't nervous. He is smiling and he seems confident. Casey does not try to hit the first pitch. He says that it isn't his style, but the umpire calls it a strike. The people watching the game in the stands are angry and shout at the umpire. Casey calms them down. Casey doesn't hit the second pitch, and it is called a strike. Now Casey looks determined. The third pitch comes. Casey swings his bat and misses the ball. He has "struck out." The game is over. Casey's team loses, and everyone in the town is sad.

| 6 | TEAM | GAME | ▲ |

Language Focus: Understanding rhyme in English, recognizing words that rhyme
Time: 10 minutes

ADJUSTING THE LEVEL
Up: After students do the activity, have them make a list of different spellings for the same sound, using the words they wrote in the activity.

Then have individual students bring into class the words from a song or poem in English that they like. On their copy, they should connect with lines the words that rhyme. They should read the songs or poems aloud in small groups.

INFORMATION GAP **Spelling**

| 7 | PARTNER | INFORMATION GAP | ↕ |

Language Focus: Learning rules for English spelling, asking for and giving information
Time: 10 minutes

ADJUSTING THE LEVEL
Down: Before students do the activity, go over the spelling rule in the box with them and provide some examples for each part of the rule:

  i before *e: friend, field*
  but not after *c: receipt*
  and not when the letters stand for an "ay" sound: *weight, veil, vein*

Up: After students do the activity, have a spelling bee with *i-e* words, using those from the activity and others. After a round or two, you may also want to include other words from the video or the *Conversation Books.*

| 8 | PARTNER | PUZZLE | ↕ |

Language Focus: Learning homonyms
Time: 10 minutes

ADJUSTING THE LEVEL
Down: Before students do the activity, discuss English homonyms. Present an example like the following and have students tell how the underlined words are alike (they sound the same), and give the meanings of the words: *I have <u>two</u> sisters. They always do things together. When one says, "I am going <u>to</u> the store, the other says, I am going, <u>too</u>."*

Up: After pairs do the activity, have them make homonym puzzles of their own.
  EXAMPLE
  pair/pear
  I need a new _____ of shoes.
  I ate a great dessert: a _____ covered with chocolate.
Here are a few examples students could use in addition to the words in the puzzle: *fare/fair; sale/sail; mail/male; plain/plane.*

PROJECT   APPENDIX 5

Poetry

| 1 | PARTNER | RESEARCH | ↕ |

Language Focus: Using English-language sources, understanding poetry
Classroom Tip: Have some poems in English available to present and discuss with students. You may want to share a few poems written by poets mentioned in the activity.
Time: 5 minutes (In addition, students do research outside of class.)

ADJUSTING THE LEVEL
Down: Present one or two poems on overheads and go through the activity with the class. Write the answers to the questions on the board. You also might suggest some short, easier poems for students to use.

Up: Have pairs write a paragraph about the author of the poem that they have chosen.

| 2 | PARTNER | PRESENTATION | ▼ |

Language Focus: Giving presentations, talking about literature
Time: 30-40 minutes

ADJUSTING THE LEVEL
Down: Have pairs make their presentations to you before they give them to the class. Make suggestions for clarifying ideas or help students with the language they need to express their ideas.

E P I S O D E
18

THE ART GALLERY

THEME Titles of Art Work

| 1 | PARTNER | GIVING TITLES | ▲ |

Language Focus: Describing pictures by giving them titles
Time: 10 minutes
Answer Key: Answers will vary.

ADJUSTING THE LEVEL
Up: Have students look through magazines or other sources and find pictures to illustrate the following ideas or some of their own:
- Peace
- Happiness/Joy
- Relaxation
- Beginnings
- Relationships

| 2 | PARTNER | DISCUSSION | ⬍ |

Language Focus: Describing pictures by giving them titles, giving reasons
Time: 10 minutes

ADJUSTING THE LEVEL
Down: Before students do the activity, have them work in small groups and describe what each picture shows. Have each group come up with two words to describe each picture and share them with the class.

Up: Have students work in pairs and write a story for one of the pictures in Activity 1. Encourage them to tell who the people in the picture are, how the situation in the picture came about, and what will happen next.

THEME Appreciating Art

| 3 | PARTNER | WAYS TO SAY IT | ▲ |

Language Focus: Expressing opinions about art, describing personal moods
Classroom Tip: School libraries often have pictures of fine art that you can sign out for classroom use. These might be helpful in the activity below.
Time: 10 minutes

ADJUSTING THE LEVEL
Up: Have students work in small groups. Ask them to bring in pictures of several paintings or works or art (or supply them with such pictures). Place the pictures on a desk or the wall of the classroom. Have the students role-play being guests at the opening of an art gallery. They are making small talk about the paintings and expressing their opinions. Write some of the following language on the board to help students in their discussions:
- Its colors are too bright/dull.
- The painting is too modern/old-fashioned.
- The painting is too abstract/too much like a photograph.
- I like representational paintings that show people and things.
- I don't like abstract paintings.

| 4 | GROUP | OPINION SURVEY | ▼ |

Language Focus: Expressing opinions, interviewing
Time: 15-20 minutes

ADJUSTING THE LEVEL
Down: Before students do the activity, work as a class to describe each picture. Discuss words to describe the mood of each picture such as *happy, sad, peaceful, full of movement, colorful, ordered, chaotic.*

THEME Money vs. Love

| 5 | GROUP | DISCUSSION | ▼ |

Language Focus: Giving personal opinions
Time: 10-15 minutes

ADJUSTING THE LEVEL
Down: Before students do the activity, go through the list as a class. Discuss the following questions for each:
- If you (buy a home) for love, what might you do?
- If you (buy a home) for money, what might you do?
  EXAMPLE
  If you buy a home for love, you buy it because there is something you really like. You might like the garden. You might like the views. You might like where the home is located.

  If you buy a home for money, you are interested in price. Maybe you think that you can sell the house for more money in the future.

Have students predict what the answer for each item will be for most students — love or money?

| 6 | GROUP | ROLE-PLAY | ⬍ |

Language Focus: Giving reasons, agreeing and disagreeing
Time: 10-15 minutes

ADJUSTING THE LEVEL
Down: Before students do the activity, ask the class to brainstorm reasons for each person in the Mendoza family to want (and not want) to sell the restaurant. Make a list with the reasons.

EXAMPLE
Mrs. Mendoza

Sell:
- We could use the extra money for retirement — my husband and I could travel or buy a house in Mexico.
- My sons could use the extra money, too. Ramón could buy a house of his own. He could have money for Alex's education.
- Alberto could use the money to invest and prepare for his future.
- Ramón could get another job where he works fewer hours.

Keep:
- The restaurant is the work of my husband's and my lifetime. We love it. We would like to see it continue.
- Ramón works here and he loves the work. He would have to look for another job if we sell.

Up: Have students do the activity twice, taking a different role each time.

GAME **Selling Something of Value**

| 7 | TEAM | GAME | ⬍ |

Language Focus: Asking yes/no questions
Time: 15-20 minutes

ADJUSTING THE LEVEL
Down: Before students play the game, go over the directions. Put the game board on an overhead, and model how to play the game with a volunteer. Brainstorm a few questions with the class.

EXAMPLE
- Does it cost more than $30,000?
- Can you put it in your living room?

Up: After students play the game several times, have them make their own list of sets of three items to sell.

Going to an Art Gallery

| 1 | GROUP | LIST | ▲ |

Language Focus: Using resources to get information, making inferences
Classroom Tip: Have some of the resources available in class (e.g., a telephone book, the newspaper, a city magazine) for students to do the activity.
Time: 15-20 minutes

ADJUSTING THE LEVEL
Up: Have groups find out about different kinds of art activities that are going on in their area and make a schedule. These might include art fairs, craft fairs, and antique shows. A local chamber of commerce might be a source of such information. Have groups post their schedules in the classroom.

| 2 | GROUP | RESEARCH | ⬍ |

Language Focus: Using interview skills
Time: 20-30 minutes (In addition, students do fieldwork outside of class.)

ADJUSTING THE LEVEL
Down: Model the activity by getting the answers to the questions for a gallery either by inviting a guest speaker from a gallery or using a brochure. From the information given, write a summary paragraph with the class.

Up: In addition to the above activity, have students write about the current exhibit at the gallery, answering questions such as these:
- What artist has works on exhibit in the gallery now?
- What style does the artist work in?
- What piece do you think is the most interesting? What does it look like?

E P I S O D E
19
THE PICNIC

THEME Having Fun

| 1 | PARTNER | INTERVIEW | ▲ |

Language Focus: Discussing leisure-time activities, interviewing
Time: 10 minutes

ADJUSTING THE LEVEL

Up: Have each student in a pair ask his/her partner follow-up questions about one of the activities. Students then write a paragraph incorporating the information he/she has found out.

> EXAMPLES
> •How often do you go to the movies?
> •What kinds of movies do you like?
> •How do you choose to go to certain movies?
> •What is the best movie you have seen lately?
>
> or
>
> •Where do you usually go on camping trips?
> •How long do you usually stay?
> •What do you do on the trips?
> •Where do you sleep?

| 2 | GROUP | OPINION SURVEY | ▲▼ |

Language Focus: Talking about everyday activities, stating preferences, interviewing
Classroom Tip: Have groups report results and find the favorite activity for the class.
Time: 10-15 minutes

ADJUSTING THE LEVEL

Down: Before students proceed, have them categorize each of the activities pictured on Page 1:
• indoor vs. outdoor
• alone vs. with others
• active vs. passive

Up: After students do the activity, have them play a guessing game with another group. They use questions like questions 1, 2, and 3 in the chart to guess a student's favorite activity.

> EXAMPLE
> •Do you like physical activities, or do you prefer to do things sitting down?
> •Do you like to do things that make you think?

Groups must guess each student's favorite activity after asking five questions. The group with the most correct answers wins.

THEME Bad Behavior

| 3 | PARTNER | INTERVIEW | ▲▼ |

Language Focus: Giving opinions
Time: 10 minutes

ADJUSTING THE LEVEL

Down: Before students do the activity, have them look up the following words in a dictionary. They should write down the words' meanings and try to think of examples of their use: *cheat, steal, gossip, lie, laugh at, litter.* Lead students in a discussion of their meanings and list examples students give on the board.

> EXAMPLE
> Students can cheat on tests. They can look at someone else's paper.

Up: Have the class share results of their ranking. Find out what the class thinks are the two "worst" behaviors and the two behaviors that they think are the "least bad."

Then have a class debate in which students defend one as the "worst" and one as the "least bad."

| 4 | GROUP | DISCUSSION | ▼ |

Language Focus: Giving opinions
Time: 10-15 minutes

ADJUSTING THE LEVEL

Down: Before students do the activity, present the following sentence frame to students to use in their answers:

If someone _____, he or she should _____.

Choose one or two topics and have students brainstorm two or three punishments.

> EXAMPLE
> If someone cheats on taxes, he or she should have to pay all the taxes, plus some extra money as a fine.

THEME Going on a Picnic

| 5 | TEAM | GAME | ▼ |

Language Focus: Describing a scene, using vocabulary related to picnics, talking about everyday activities
Time: 10 minutes

ADJUSTING THE LEVEL

Down: Adjust the time of the activity for the students. Instead of ten minutes for all three categories, give students five minutes for the first category and then review the answers. Follow the same procedure for the second and third categories. This way students get a chance to discuss words they might be able to use in the next category.

After students do the activity, have them work in pairs and make a word web for picnics. They should use the three categories from the activity, writing each in a large circle. They should write all the words they can think of relating to the category on lines coming out of the circle. (See Episode 23, page 1, for an example of a word web.)

Getting Close to Someone

Team Games

| 6 | PARTNER | INFORMATION GAP | ⬍ |

Language Focus: Asking for and giving information, talking about everyday activities
Time: 10-15 minutes

ADJUSTING THE LEVEL

Down: Before students do the activity, write a list of questions similar to those in the activity on the board.

EXAMPLE
- What do you usually do on Saturdays?
- What sport do you like to play?
- What do you like to read?
- Where do you like to go on vacation?
- What kind of movies do you like to see?
- What is your favorite kind of food?
- What are you good at doing?

Have students ask you some of the questions. Then have different members of the class ask questions of volunteers.

Up: Have students role-play a conversation between two people who don't know each other very well. They can answer the questions for themselves or take on a different identity. Here are some scenarios:
- You work in the same office with someone but you have never spoken to the person other than to say hello. The person is sitting next to you in the cafeteria.
- You go to the same school. You see someone waiting for the same bus.
- You are on the beach. Someone is reading the same book you are.

| 1 | GROUP | RESEARCH | ⬍ |

Language Focus: Using sources to get information, using sports vocabulary
Classroom Tip: Have available books about sports, particularly ones written in simple English and ones with illustrations. You might also want to have relevant volumes of encyclopedias available.
Time: 5-10 minutes (In addition, students do research outside of class.)

ADJUSTING THE LEVEL

Down: Before students do the activity, model how to do it using baseball as the sport. If possible, put an article about baseball from an encyclopedia on an overhead and help students find the answers to the questions.

If possible, have available picture dictionaries that show various sports actions. Have students identify those actions that are part of each of the sports.

Up: Have students add at least five additional questions to answer.

EXAMPLE
- What is the size of the field, court, etc., on which the game is played?
- What are the names of the positions in the game?
- Is the game divided by time? What are the divisions?
- How long is each?
- Are there referees in the game? What do they do?

| 2 | GROUP | POSTER | ⬍ |

Language Focus: Writing a paragraph about sports, reporting information in written form
Classroom Tip: You may want to provide groups with a large piece of paper on which to make their posters. In addition, if students are working on the posters in class, have colored markers and pencils and crayons available.
Time: 40-60 minutes (Students may prepare their posters outside of class time.)

ADJUSTING THE LEVEL

Down: Model how to write a paragraph, using the information about baseball discussed in Activity 1.

Up: Have students make presentations about their favorite sports and tell of any personal knowledge or experience with them.

E P I S O D E
20
PREJUDICE

THEME Apologizing

1	PARTNER	WAYS TO SAY IT	

Language Focus: Apologizing
Time: 10 minutes

ADJUSTING THE LEVEL
Down: Go over ways to apologize. Then have students work in groups of three. Present a situation (such as those listed below) orally. Within the groups, each student apologizes in two different ways, using expressions from the list in Activity 1.

> EXAMPLE
> • You borrow your sister's tape player without asking.
> • You forgot to return a call to your friend.
> • You lose a book a friend lent you.

Up: Have students do a role-play of at least six exchanges based on one of the situations. Present expressions for accepting apologies, such as *That's OK, but don't do it next time.*, or *It's no big deal.*

THEME
Teaching Children Right from Wrong

2	GROUP	RANKING	

Language Focus: Giving opinions
Time: 10-15 minutes

ADJUSTING THE LEVEL
Down: Before students do the activity, discuss the following questions as a class:
- What are some things you think are wrong for people to do?
- Think back to when you were a child. How did you first learn these things were wrong?

After students do the activity, discuss each item. Have students who ranked an item 1 or 2 tell why they ranked the item so high.

3	PARTNER	MATCHING	

Language Focus: Understanding proverbs, giving opinions
Time: 10-15 minutes
Answer Key: 1. c, 2. e, 3. a, 4. d, 5. b

ADJUSTING THE LEVEL
Up: Have students do one or more of these activities:
1. Rank the proverbs from the most useful to the least useful.

2. Discuss the role of physical punishment in raising children. Is it a good idea? Is it a bad idea?
3. Answer this question: What is the best advice you have for teaching children about right and wrong?

THEME Appreciating Differences

4	GROUP	SURVEY	

Language Focus: Giving personal information, finding differences and similarities, making comparisons
Time: 10-15 minutes

ADJUSTING THE LEVEL
Down: Before students do the activity, have them generate sentences orally for a category you state: one student makes a statement, and another student responds with a statement that indicates a difference or a similarity.

> EXAMPLES
> S1: I like ice cream for dessert.
> S2: I like fruit for dessert.
> S1: I like ice cream for dessert, but Paula likes fruit for dessert.
>
> or
>
> S1: I like ice cream for dessert.
> S2: I like ice cream for dessert.
> S1: Both Mario and I like ice cream for dessert.

Possible categories to use:
- home country
- number of brothers and sisters
- ability to play a sport
- ability to work with computers
- places visited
- favorite foods

Up: As students do the activity, have them find at least five similarities and five differences with respect to each group member.

5	GROUP	DISCUSSION	

Language Focus: Making comparisons, identifying categories
Time: 10-15 minutes

ADJUSTING THE LEVEL
Down: Before groups do the activity, have volunteers read aloud sentences from Activity 4. Have students say how the two students are alike or different, using a category.

> EXAMPLE
> Marta and Paul are different. They come from different countries.
> Marta and Mario are alike. They come from the same country.

6	GROUP	DISCUSSION	

Language Focus: Giving opinions
Time: 10-15 minutes

ADJUSTING THE LEVEL
Down: Find two pictures that show people who are dressed

differently; for example, someone in a conservative business suit and someone dressed in the latest extreme style. Before students do the activity, show them the pictures. Have them discuss these questions:

- In what ways can it be good to feel different from other people? How do people show they are different?
- In what ways is it bad to feel different from other people?
- Do you think people are really all the same at heart? Why?

THEME **Prejudice in the U.S.**

7 | GROUP | DISCUSSION | ▼

Language Focus: Making generalizations, discussing personal experiences or knowledge
Time: 10-15 minutes

ADJUSTING THE LEVEL
Down: To make the activity more concrete, ask the class to list common kinds of behaviors that show prejudice.

> EXAMPLE
> *Race:* People can't eat in certain restaurants. People can't get good jobs. People can't get into certain clubs.
> *People with disabilities:* People in wheelchairs can't use buses or other kinds of public transportation. They are not considered for certain jobs.

8 | PARTNER | INFORMATION GAP | ▲▼

Language Focus: Asking for and giving information
Classroom Tip: Have available some sources of information on Martin Luther King, Jr., such as encyclopedia articles, books, or old newspaper articles.
Time: 10 minutes

ADJUSTING THE LEVEL
Down: Before students do the activity, write a sample puzzle on the board so that students understand the activity. Write an alphabet code, using number and letters, like the one in the book (but not the same). Write a short sentence in the code for the students to decipher. After students do the activity, present some basic information on Martin Luther King, Jr.

Up: Have students work in small groups to find out some basic information about who Martin Luther King, Jr., was and why he is important in U.S. history. Have groups share paragraphs.

PROJECT APPENDIX 8

Greeting Cards

1 | PARTNER | RESEARCH | ▲

Language Focus: Getting information, understanding the language of greeting cards
Classroom Tip: Have pairs report their findings to the class.
Time: 10 minutes (In addition, students do research outside of class. You may want to allow time for students to report what they learned.)

ADJUSTING THE LEVEL
Up: For four or five types of cards, have students write a typical message that would be found in that type of card. Ask them to describe an example of a card they liked or they thought was funny or unusual.

They can write their results in chart form and compare them with other pairs.

2 | GROUP | SURVEY | ▲▼

Language Focus: Using interview skills
Classroom Tip: After the activity is finished, have groups report results and add up the votes to find overall results for the class.
Time: 10-15 minutes (In addition, students do fieldwork outside of class.)

ADJUSTING THE LEVEL
Down: Have students answer these questions:
- When was the last time you sent a greeting card? What kind of card was it?
- When was the last time you received a greeting card? What kind of card was it?

Have students review the kinds of cards they found in Activity 1. Have them tell what kinds of cards they receive and send.

Up: Have students discuss why they send cards for certain occasions. If some students never send cards, have them discuss their reasons for not doing so.

Have students discuss cultural differences they know between their country and the United States with regard to responding to certain events. For example, what is an appropriate response when someone in a friend's family dies?

EPISODE
21
A DIFFICULT DECISION

THEME A Daily Schedule

Language Focus: Talking about daily schedules, using the present tense
Time: 10-15 minutes

ADJUSTING THE LEVEL
Up: Have students do the same activity for the weekends — both Saturday and Sunday. Then have three pairs get together and share schedules. Have them try to list at least three similarities and three differences among the schedules (e.g., *We all get up before 10:00 on Saturdays.*). Have groups share their lists with the entire class.

| 2 | GROUP | SURVEY | ▼ |

Language Focus: Giving personal information, giving opinions
Classroom Tip: After the activity is finished, have groups report results and add up the votes to find overall results for the class.
Time: 10-15 minutes

ADJUSTING THE LEVEL
Down: Provide students with the following phrases, pointing to the differences in meaning:

All of	100%
Most of	From about 51-99%
Many of	From about 40-70%
Some of	From about 5-30%
A few of	5% to 10%
None of	0%

Have students use the language to write a summary of the results for their group.

> EXAMPLE
> Most of the students in the group think that their schedule is too busy.
>
> None of the students in the group thinks that their schedule is very flexible.

THEME Being Stubborn

| 3 | CLASS | BRAINSTORM | ▲▼ |

Language Focus: Giving reasons
Time: 10-15 minutes

ADJUSTING THE LEVEL
Down: Before students do the activity, review and discuss events that happened in the series. As a class, talk about the reasons that Mr. Wang gives for wanting to take Vincent out of the program and the reasons Emma and Rebecca give for keeping him in.

Up: In groups, have students brainstorm at least three reasons that Mr. Wang might give for wanting to take Vincent out of the after-school program and that Emma might give for wanting Vincent to stay in the program. Then have the group prepare a role-play between Emma Washington and Mr. Wang. Each character gives some of the reasons discussed. Each group presents its role-play to the class.

| 4 | PARTNER | ROLE-PLAY | ▼ |

Language Focus: Using persuasive language
Time: 10 minutes

ADJUSTING THE LEVEL
Down: Write some common language for persuading and refusing/declining on the board:

> *Persuading:*
> Why don't you _____?
> Oh, come on.
> You should _____.
> I am sure that you will/we will/I will _____.
> Let's _____.
>
> *Refusing:*
> I really don't want to _____.
> I don't feel like _____. (gerund)
> It will be better if I/we _____.
> Thanks anyway.

Model the activity. Choose one of the situations in the activity, and have the class brainstorm reasons for both characters to give. Write the reasons down and then use them in a model conversation.

> EXAMPLE
> Driving — to stop or not to stop
>
> *Reasons to stop:* I'm hungry now./You need to rest so that you won't get too tired. It's safer./If we don't stop, there isn't another restaurant for 25 miles./We are in no hurry.
>
> *Reasons to go on:* I'm not hungry./If we go on, we can reach a big city. Then we find a hotel and eat in the same place./It's better to drive when it is light out.

5 | PARTNER | SHARING | ▼

Language Focus: Asking for and giving information, describing people
Time: 20-30 minutes

ADJUSTING THE LEVEL

Down: Model the activity by having students ask you the questions. Write your answers on the board. With the class, compose a paragraph about the person you miss.

GAME **Solving Problems**

6 | CLASS | GAME | ▲▼

Language Focus: Giving advice
Time: 20-30 minutes

ADJUSTING THE LEVEL

Down: Provide students with language for stating problems and giving advice.

> EXAMPLE
> *Stating problems:*
> Can you help me?/What should I do?/What do you think I should do?
>
> *Giving advice:*
> You should _____/ You might _____/ It would be a good idea for you to _____.

Up: Have each student brainstorm two solutions to each problem. When students play the game, they pick two solution cards, and each student needs to find two solutions to his/her problem.

PROJECT

Making Decisions

1 | GROUP | SURVEY | ▼

Language Focus: Using interview skills
Time: 5-10 minutes (In addition, students do fieldwork outside of class.)

ADJUSTING THE LEVEL

Down: To prepare for doing the task, have students do the interview first as a class activity, asking you and/or other students the questions. In this way, students become familiar with vocabulary and the meaning of the questions.

2 | GROUP | DATA ANALYSIS | ▼

Language Focus: Making generalizations, making comparisons
Time: 10-15 minutes

ADJUSTING THE LEVEL

Down: Copy on the board the phrases from Activity 2 in this episode (see "Adjusting the Level"). Tell each student to use the terms to make generalizations about the information they gather in Part B of this activity.

> EXAMPLE
> Most of the people mentioned decisions about money.
> Many of the people mentioned decisions about children.

EPISODE
22
GUITAR LESSONS

THEME **Marriage**

| 1 | GROUP | DISCUSSION | ▲ |

Language Focus: Giving opinions
Time: 10-15 minutes

ADJUSTING THE LEVEL
Up: After groups do the activity, have them rank the items for a successful marriage in order, from most important (1) to least important (8). Have groups share their rankings with other groups.

| 2 | CLASS | BRAINSTORM | ▲ |

Language Focus: Giving opinions about successful marriages
Time: 5-10 minutes

ADJUSTING THE LEVEL
Up: To make the activity more difficult, have students do it in pairs and then share their lists with the class. Then have volunteers tell about successful marriages they know and what they think makes them a success.

| 3 | GROUP | DEBATE | ⬍ |

Language Focus: Giving reasons, using persuasive language
Time: 15-20 minutes

ADJUSTING THE LEVEL
Down: Before students do the activity, review the events on the videotape. Ask: *What is Ramón's family situation?* Then, with the class, brainstorm two reasons for each position.
Position 1:
• Just because a first marriage is not successful doesn't mean a second marriage won't be a success.
• A new wife could help Ramón in raising Alex.
Position 2:
• Alex's life has seen many changes. It is best for Ramón to give him some security.
• Ramón is too busy to work on a relationship right now.

Up: After students do the activity, have them work in pairs and role-play giving Ramón the advice the class thought was best.

THEME **Accepting a Gift**

| 4 | PARTNER | DISCUSSION | ▼ |

Language Focus: Giving opinions
Time: 10 minutes

ADJUSTING THE LEVEL
Down: Before students do the activity, have them discuss the answers to these questions:
1. Who do you mostly give as gifts to (family members, friends, teachers, people at work)?
2. On what occasions do you give gifts?
3. What do you think is an appropriate amount of money to spend on a gift for family members (friends, etc.)?
Then have students think of situations where they think it might be wrong to give expensive gifts.

After students do the activity, explain that in the United States most people would answer the questions in this way: *1. No 2. Yes 3. No 4. Yes 5. Yes.* Have them discuss any differences in their home countries/cultures.

| 5 | PARTNER | WAYS TO SAY IT | ⬍ |

Language Focus: Expressing thanks for a gift
Time: 10-15 minutes

ADJUSTING THE LEVEL
Down: Go over the expressions in the box with students. Have them each write the names of two gifts, each on a separate piece of paper (or they could cut pictures of "gifts" from magazines). Have them work in small groups and practice exchanging the "gifts" with one another. Suggest that they present the gifts by saying *I have a gift for you.,* or *I want you to accept this gift.*

Up: Have students each choose one of the situations and write a thank-you note to the person who sent the gift. You may want to model how to write a thank-you note: it usually includes mention of the gift and how it will be used.

THEME **Children and Homework**

| 6 | CLASS | POLL | ▲ |

Language Focus: Giving opinions
Time: 10-15 minutes

ADJUSTING THE LEVEL
Up: Have students write paragraphs about their childhood experiences with homework. They should try to answer these questions:
• How much homework did you get?
• Did you always do your homework?
• Did you like to do homework?
• Do you think that doing homework helped you learn?
Have students share their paragraphs in small groups.

```
7    TEAM    GAME                          ⬍
```

Language Focus: Giving reasons
Time: 10-15 minutes

ADJUSTING THE LEVEL
Down: Before students do the activity, brainstorm two reasons for each position.

    EXAMPLE
    Position 1:
    •Homework helps children practice what they are learning.
    •Homework makes children responsible.

    Position 2:
    •Children should spend time playing with other children, not at home with books.
    •The time at school is enough for children to learn what they need to.

Up: After students do the activity, have them form groups and debate these two positions:
  • Children should have homework to do every day
  • Children should not have homework to do every day

INFORMATION GAP **Favors for Friends**

```
8    PARTNER    INFORMATION GAP             ⬇
```

Language Focus: Asking for favors, giving information
Time: 10-15 minutes

ADJUSTING THE LEVEL
Down: Model the language for asking for favors by writing the following on the board:
  • Can you help me?
  • Could you (drive me home after class)?
  • Would you (help me with my homework)?
Model a situation like those in the boxes on pages 5 and 6.

    EXAMPLE
    I need to bring a box of books to class and my car isn't working. I need someone to go the library, get the books, and bring the books to class tomorrow. You will need a car to do this favor for me because there are a lot of books! Can you help me?

Have individual students tell why they could or could not help you. List language to use on the board:

    I am sorry I can't. I have to _____ at _____.
    But I am free at _____.
or
    OK. I am free. I can help you.

    Next, have Student As work in pairs and Student Bs work in different pairs. Each person reads over the situation in the box and explains it to his/her partner before starting the activity.

Television

```
1    GROUP    SURVEY                        ⬆
```

Language Focus: Discussing personal habits, making predictions, using interview skills
Time: 10-15 minutes over two class periods (In addition, students do fieldwork outside of class.)

ADJUSTING THE LEVEL
Up: Have groups prepare a report with total results. Suggest that they use pie graphs for items 1, 4, and 5, and bar graphs for items 2 and 3. Tell them also to include raw figures.

    Then have each student write a commentary about the results, answering these questions:
  • Do you think that people watch too much television?
  • Which of the results surprised you?

    Have groups share results. Ask volunteers to prepare graphs that incorporate information from all the groups. Have the class discuss the results.

E P I S O D E
23

THE RETIREMENT PARTY

THEME Moving Away

Language Focus: Giving reasons
Time: 10 minutes

ADJUSTING THE LEVEL
Down: As a class, discuss the situation with Ramón, Alex, and Ramón's ex-wife, Christine. What is happening? Then brainstorm two reasons for each position to help get students started with the activity.

EXAMPLE
Position 1:
•Alex needs a mother. He should be with her.
•Ramón is too busy to care for Alex. It is better that Alex go with his mother.

Position 2:
•Alex lives with his father. Alex doesn't need another change in his life.
•Alex's friends are in San Francisco. It will be hard for him to leave them.

Up: After students do the activity, have students work in pairs and make a role-play between Ramón and his ex-wife, Christine. Ramón tells why it is best for Alex to stay, and Christine tells why it is best for Alex to move.

| 2 | CLASS | GAME | ▲ |

Language Focus: Using place-names
Classroom Tip: Have a large map of the world or a world atlas available.
Time: 10 minutes

ADJUSTING THE LEVEL
Up: As students play the game, you might have them locate each place on a world map.
Have students play again, this time with the names of cities.

| 3 | PARTNER | INTERVIEW | ↕ |

Language Focus: Talking about personal experiences, giving opinions
Classroom Tip: Have pairs share responses.
Time: 10-15 minutes

ADJUSTING THE LEVEL
Down: Before students do the activity, have them ask you the questions. Have volunteers write your answers on the board.

Up: Have students continue to interview their partners to get enough information to write a paragraph on one of the following topics:
  • A Time My Partner Moved
  • Where My Partner Would Like to Live and Why

| 4 | PARTNER | STORYTELLING | ▼ |

Language Focus: Telling a story
Time: 20-30 minutes (This can be extended over several class periods as students present their stories.)
Answer Key: beach #3, moving #2, invention #1

ADJUSTING THE LEVEL
Down: To guide pairs in their storytelling, write the following questions on the board and suggest that they try to answer them in their story:
  • Who is the person?
  • What did the person invent?
  • What did the person get as a result?
  • What did the person do then?
  • Where did the person go to live?
  • What is the person's life like now?
  • How did the person's life change?

THEME Disciplining Children

| 5 | PARTNER | BRAINSTORM | ▼ |

Language Focus: Talking about common experiences, giving opinions
Time: 10-15 minutes

ADJUSTING THE LEVEL
Down: As a class, brainstorm ways that students are disciplined (being hit, not being able to go out with friends, being told to go to one's room, being given extra chores). Then have students discuss which methods of discipline they think are used most or not used at all in their cultures.

| 6 | CLASS | DEBATE | ↕ |

Language Focus: Giving opinions
Time: 15-20 minutes

ADJUSTING THE LEVEL
Down: With the class, brainstorm two reasons for each position.

EXAMPLE
Position 1:
- Sometimes reasoning with children just doesn't work.
- Physical punishment lets children know that you are serious.

Position 2:
- Physical punishment shows anger. You should discipline children with calmness.
- Physical punishment does not help children see why their behavior was wrong.

Up: After students do the activity, have them work in groups and come up with an argument against the "best reason" for each opinion. Have groups share arguments.

THEME Retirement

| 7 | PARTNER | INTERVIEW | ⬍ |

Language Focus: Giving personal preferences
Time: 10 minutes

ADJUSTING THE LEVEL
Down: Have the class brainstorm a list of activities that people commonly pursue when they retire.

EXAMPLE
go fishing, write a book, travel to foreign countries, visit grandchildren

Ask students to identify and discuss any differences in activities based on culture.

Up: Have each student write a paragraph about what an ideal retirement would be for him/her and share the paragraph with his/her partner.

| 8 | GROUP | DISCUSSION | ⬍ |

Language Focus: Giving opinions, discussing jobs
Time: 10-15 minutes

ADJUSTING THE LEVEL
Down: As a class, brainstorm the list of jobs people over 65 should not do, and tell why each is not recommended.

EXAMPLE
airplane pilot — they need keen senses and reflexes
mover — the work is physically very difficult

Up: Have students explain why they think each job is not appropriate. Have groups share their lists. Have the class note the most common jobs on each of the two lists.

Have students discuss their opinions about retirement. Are there differences in retirement ages among their countries? Do they think that there should be laws about retirement?

GAME Gossip

| 9 | TEAM | GAME | ⬍ |

Language Focus: Talking about oneself
Time: 15-20 minutes

ADJUSTING THE LEVEL
Down: As students prepare cards, have them work in pairs. The partners should discuss their personal experiences for a few minutes. The partners help one another choose what to put on their cards. You might want to pair students of higher and lower language proficiency. Also, these pairs should then play on the same team.

Up: After students do the activity, have them list the most surprising things they learned about their classmates.

PROJECT   APPENDIX 11

International Celebrations

| 1 | GROUP | RESEARCH | ▼ |

Language Focus: Talking about culture/customs, getting information from various sources
Time: 5-10 minutes (In addition, students do research outside of class.)

ADJUSTING THE LEVEL
Down: Model the activity by having students interview you about the holiday and country of your choice. Have volunteers write the answers on the board.

| 2 | CLASS | PARTY | ⬍ |

Language Focus: Talking about culture/customs, planning events
Classroom Tip: Plan with the class what needs to be done to prepare for the party. For example, you might want to have large tables available in the classroom or something on which to play music.
Time: 30-45 minutes (Allow class time for students to plan their group activities, as well as for the actual party.)

ADJUSTING THE LEVEL
Down: Work with each group to plan what it will do for the celebration, using the information that it has on customs/culture. You may want to arrange for a person from the country in question to act as a resource person.

Up: Have each group explain to the class its part in the celebration (e.g., describe the food, the meaning of the decorations, etc.).

EPISODE 24

THE PHONE CALL

THEME **Parties**

Language Focus: Talking about everyday activities, discussing preferences, interviewing
Time: 15 minutes

ADJUSTING THE LEVEL
Up: Have each group prepare a report with the results. You may suggest that groups prepare a bar graph with the activities on the bottom and a separate bar for men and women. Have groups compare their results with other groups and prepare a class graph on the board.

| 2 | TEAM | GAME | ▲▼ |

Language Focus: Talking about everyday activities
Time: 10 minutes

ADJUSTING THE LEVEL
Down: As students do the activity, have dictionaries available to check spellings. To prompt students' thinking, suggest that they think of more things to do related to music (singing songs, playing instruments) or conversations with people.

Up: Have students do a follow-up activity. Have each student list two or three kinds of parties that are common in their countries and describe what people do (and do not do) at the parties. Have students work in groups and compare lists.

| 3 | PARTNER | GAME | ▼ |

Language Focus: Asking yes/no questions
Time: 15 minutes

ADJUSTING THE LEVEL
Down: Before students do the activity, brainstorm a list of questions to ask.
> EXAMPLE
> • Is the person living?
> • Is the person a woman?
> • Is the person from the United States?
> • Is the person in politics?
> • Is the person in the entertainment business?

Then model the game: pick a famous person, write down the person's name on a slip of paper, and have students ask you questions.

THEME **Cheer Up!**

| 4 | CLASS | BRAINSTORM | ▲ |

Language Focus: Talking about everyday activities
Time: 5-10 minutes

ADJUSTING THE LEVEL
Up: Have students write a paragraph about a time when someone cheered them up. You might give them a list of questions like the following to guide their writing:
• What was the problem? Why were you sad?
• What did the person do to cheer you up?
• What did the person say?
• What did you say or do in response?
• How did you feel after you talked to the person?

| 5 | GROUP | INTERVIEW | ▲▼ |

Language Focus: Talking about everyday activities, interviewing
Time: 10-15 minutes

ADJUSTING THE LEVEL
Down: Before students do the activity, brainstorm a list of common things that people do to cheer themselves up and write the list on the board.
> EXAMPLE
> •go to the movies
> •go to a restaurant
> •eat something special
> •play some special music
> •buy something you've wanted for a long time

Up: Have groups share lists with the class and come up with a list of the ten most common answers. Have students discuss any answers that they think are really good and any that they think are bad.

| 6 | PARTNER | GREETING CARD | ▲▼ |

Language Focus: Giving people encouragement, writing greeting cards
Classroom Tip: Have colored markers, pencils, crayons, and colored paper available for students to make cards. In addition, you might want to have some examples of friendship cards to show students.
Time: 15-20 minutes

ADJUSTING THE LEVEL
Down: If possible, show the class examples of cards designed to cheer up friends. With the class, brainstorm greetings for friends.
> EXAMPLE
> •Remember, through good times or bad, I am your friend. You can count on me.
> •Rain or shine, you can count on me to be your umbrella.

Up: Have students write a note to a friend who is in need of cheering up because he/she broke up with boyfriend or girlfriend or because he/she lost a job.

THEME Bad News

| 7 | PARTNER | WAYS TO SAY IT | ⬍ |

Language Focus: Giving bad news
Time: 10-15 minutes

ADJUSTING THE LEVEL
Down: Point out the pattern in the language in the exercise by writing the following sentence frames on the board:

> I have some bad news and some good news. The bad news is _____. The good news is _____.

Up: Have students choose one of the situations and act out a role-play, with one telling another the news.

GAME Making a Toast

| 8 | GROUP | GAME | ⬍ |

Language Focus: Making toasts
Time: 15-20 minutes (Students can play the game several times.)

ADJUSTING THE LEVEL
Down: Review the toasts that Alberto and Ramón give for their parents at the party, either by showing the video or by having students discuss what they remember. Brainstorm the list of occasions for toasts with the class instead of in groups.

> EXAMPLE
> • at a wedding
> • at a retirement party
> • at a party where a famous person is the guest of honor
> • at a birthday party
> • at a graduation

Then model making toasts for some of the situations. Write the formulas for toasts given on page 6 on the board:

> I'd like to propose a toast _____.

> Here's to _____.

> Let's toast _____.

Then present some examples of toasts for different occasions.

> EXAMPLE
> Here's to my sister on her wedding. She was always there when I really needed help and she always helped with a smile. I wish you much success in your marriage.

Up: As a follow-up activity, have students pretend that a famous person is coming to a banquet at your school. Each student writes a toast for the celebrity.

PROJECT   APPENDIX 12

Dancing

| 1 | PARTNER | RESEARCH | ⬍ |

Language Focus: Describing everyday activities, using sources to get information
Time: 10 minutes (In addition, students do research outside of class.)

ADJUSTING THE LEVEL
Down: Have students describe dances they know. You might want them to demonstrate the dance. Then as a class, come up with ways to the describe the dance and write a description on the board.

Up: If possible, have students add one or more of the following items to their descriptions:
1. A description of the steps in the dance
2. A history of the dance
3. Costumes worn for the dance
4. Music for the dance

| 2 | PARTNER | POSTER | ⬍ |

Language Focus: Making an oral presentation, reporting information in written form
Time: 20-30 minutes (The time is for pair presentations, which can be spread over several class sessions. You might also want to allow class time for partners to prepare their posters.)

ADJUSTING THE LEVEL
Down: Have pairs make their presentation to you before they present it to the class. Provide suggestions for clarification and improvement.

Up: Have students include some of the items listed for Activity 1 in their posters or presentations.

EPISODE 25

REBECCA REMEMBERS

THEME Having Regrets

1 | PARTNER | MATCHING | ▲

Language Focus: Discussing regrets, giving advice
Time: 5-10 minutes
Answer Key: 1. c, 2. e, 3. d, 4. b, 5. a

ADJUSTING THE LEVEL
Up: Have pairs choose one of the situations and act out a role-play of at least six exchanges. They should give background information and try to expand the advice.

> EXAMPLE
> A: You know, I was thinking all weekend. I should have taken that job. I think I was just afraid to try something new.
> B: Call and see if you can still accept the job.
> A: They probably already hired someone else.
> B: Well, you can try. What have you got to lose? (and so on)

2 | PARTNER | ROLE-PLAY | ▼

Language Focus: Discussing regrets, giving advice
Time: 10-15 minutes

ADJUSTING THE LEVEL
Down: Before students do the activity, brainstorm a list of common regrets.

> EXAMPLE
> •I should have taken computer courses.
> •I should have saved more money.
> •I shouldn't have spent so much time watching TV.

Point out the language that begins each regret:
> •*I should have* + past participle
> •*I shouldn't have* + past participle

Then have students brainstorm advice for some of the regrets.

THEME Remembering Good and Bad Times

3 | PARTNER | SHARING | ↕

Language Focus: Discussing personal experiences
Time: 15-20 minutes

ADJUSTING THE LEVEL
Down: Before students do the activity, have the class brainstorm possible situations to use in the activity (e.g., parties, weddings, a trip, leaving a home, losing a friend).

Up: Have students do the activity for both a good and a bad time.

4 | CLASS | GUESSING | ↕

Language Focus: Discussing personal experiences
Time: 15-20 minutes

ADJUSTING THE LEVEL
Down: Model how to write a paragraph about a good or bad time. Do one of the following:
* Share an experience with the class. Then, as a class write a paragraph that describes the experience.
* Choose one of Rebecca's experiences for the class to write about. Write the paragraph from Rebecca's viewpoint, using "I."
  EXAMPLE
  Good experiences: Going out with Alberto to see San Francisco, working with the children at the after-school program
  Bad experience: Being rejected by music schools

Up: As suggested for Activity 3, have students write about both good and bad experiences. Or allow students to write about one of their classmate's experiences that has been shared with them.

THEME Mixed Feelings

5 | GROUP | DISCUSSION | ▼

Language Focus: Discussing personal experiences and feelings
Time: 15-20 minutes

ADJUSTING THE LEVEL
Down: With the class, fill in a model chart. Use the situation of someone who is moving to a new country to go to school. Write down possible feelings for the columns at the left and right.

Then, with the class, brainstorm a list of possible events over which people could have mixed feelings, such as changing jobs, moving someplace new, making a big purchase. The purpose is to help students think of situations they might write about.

Language Focus: Giving opinions
Time: 10-15 minutes

ADJUSTING THE LEVEL

Down: Before students do the task, go over the statements in the activity. With the class, think of one reason people might agree or disagree with each statement.

Up: Have each group list five more important issues over which people would agree or disagree. Tell them to include the word *should* in each statement. Have the groups present their issues to the class, and have the students raise their hands to indicate whether they agree, disagree, or have mixed feelings about the issue.

| 7 | CLASS | DEBATE | ▼ |

Language Focus: Giving reasons
Time: 20-25 minutes

ADJUSTING THE LEVEL

Down: Before students do the activity, have a class discussion about the chosen debate topic. Bring in newspaper or magazine articles or any background information you can find. Share these with the class and discuss them. This will help students prepare their reasons for the debate.

GAME Life Lessons

| 8 | GROUP | GAME | ⬦ |

Language Focus: Discussing personal experiences, giving advice
Time: 20-30 minutes (Students can play the game several times in the course of the episode.)

ADJUSTING THE LEVEL

Down: Before students play the game, have them go over the sample life experiences on the game board and in the examples. Then, with the class, brainstorm several life experiences and lessons learned. Have students work in pairs to prepare the game cards. You might want to pair students of lower language proficiency with those of higher language proficiency.

Up: After students play the game, have them write a paragraph about a recent life lesson they have learned. Have students share their paragraphs in small groups, and have the group members discuss whether they have had similar experiences.

PROJECT   APPENDIX 1

Family Obligations

| 1 | PARTNER | SURVEY | ⬦ |

Language Focus: Discussing family obligations, using interview skills
Time: 10 minutes (In addition, students do fieldwork outside of class.)

ADJUSTING THE LEVEL

Down: Before students interview people outside of class, have them ask you and several other class members the questions. Write results on the board. Keep the results so that students can compare them with the results from their interviews.

Up: Have students work in small groups. They should discuss the family obligations they each have. Have them determine if there are differences by birth order, sex, or country of origin.

| 2 | GROUP | DATA ANALYSIS | ⬦ |

Language Focus: Making generalizations
Time: 10-20 minutes

ADJUSTING THE LEVEL

Down: To guide students in making generalizations, write the following sentences on the board and ask students to use them in their discussions. (Tell students to put *oldest, middle, youngest,* or *only* in the blank before the word *child.*)

1. In our group, the person with the most checks has _____ checks. This person is the _____ child in the family.
2. In our group, the person with the second-highest number of checks has _____ checks. This person is the _____ child in the family.
3. In our group, the two people with most checks are the _____ child (and the _____ child).
   or
   In our group, the two people with the most checks are the _____ child and the _____ child in the family.

Up: Have groups write a report on their findings to share with the people they interviewed or with other classes. Have them discuss:
- what the most family obligations are
- which child — oldest, middle, youngest, or only — takes family responsibilities the most seriously

EPISODE
26

THE EMERGENCY

THEME **Airports**

| 1 | TEAM | GAME | ▲ |

Language Focus: Using and spelling geographic names
Classroom Tip: Have available atlases or other maps of the world written in English.
Time: 20 minutes

ADJUSTING THE LEVEL
Up: To make the activity more challenging, have students also list the country in which the airport is located. In addition, tell students they will get a point for each additional international airport, city, and country they can name.

Have students say the names of cities and countries. Encourage them to use dictionaries for help with pronunciation. Then have a "spelling bee." Name an airport. Students have to name the city and country in which the airport is located or they are out of the game.

| 2 | GROUP | SURVEY | ⬍ |

Language Focus: Discussing personal experiences, using the present perfect
Time: 15-20 minutes

ADJUSTING THE LEVEL
Down: To model the activity, tell your responses to the statements in the activity. Recount any interesting personal experiences. Have the class discuss similar experiences.

After doing the activity, each student can write a list of things that he/she has done in an airport and share it with the group. Write the following sentence frame on the board:
I have + past participle + at an airport.

EXAMPLE
  •I have bought presents at an airport.
  •I have waited five hours at an airport.
  •I have missed a flight at an airport.

Up: As students answer items 1 and 2, encourage them to give reasons for their opinions.

After students discuss their experiences in Part B, have each group member retell the most interesting experiences to someone from a different group.

THEME **Cleaning the House**

| 3 | PARTNER | RANKING | ▲ |

Language Focus: Discussing everyday activities, giving opinions
Classroom Tip: After students do the activity, you may want to tally results to find the housecleaning job that students dislike the most.
Time: 10 minutes

ADJUSTING THE LEVEL
Up: Have pairs play a game. Ask them to brainstorm as many additional household tasks as they can think of in five minutes (e.g., cooking, feeding pets, doing laundry). With the class, make a master list of tasks, writing them on the board. Pairs get one point for every answer, plus an additional point for every answer that wasn't on anyone else's list. The pair with the most points wins.

| 4 | PARTNER | MAKING A LIST | ▼ |

Language Focus: Discussing common household tasks, using commands
Time: 10 minutes

ADJUSTING THE LEVEL
Down: Before students do the activity, have them act out the verbs that are listed in the box.

THEME **First Aid**

| 5 | PARTNER | MATCHING | ⬍ |

Language Focus: Reading directions, using vocabulary related to first aid
Time: 10-15 minutes
Answer Key: burn, bloody nose, cut, sting, sprain

ADJUSTING THE LEVEL
Down: Have students first study the vocabulary at the top and in the box at the left. Then give brief definitions such as the following and have students name the items:
  • This happens when a bee bites you. (sting)
  • This can happen when you get too near a stove. (burn)
  • This can happen when you are using a knife. (cut)
  • You can put this on a burn to make it cool. (ice)
  • You put this on a cut after it has stopped bleeding. (bandage)

Up: Have each student carefully read over one of the sets of directions. Have him or her recount what to do for that kind of first aid.
  EXAMPLE
  When you have a burn, you should put the area under a faucet. You should run cold water over the burn for several minutes. You can take a painkiller such as aspirin.

You can also ask students to share any home remedies they may have for these or any other first aid situations.

6	PARTNER	INFORMATION GAP	↕

Language Focus: Discussing medical emergencies, describing a scene, asking for and giving information
Time: 15-20 minutes
Answer Key: Here are the differences:

1. The doctor in Picture A is looking at an x-ray of a chest; the doctor in Picture B is looking at an x-ray of a leg.
2. The nurse at the left in Picture A is giving the boy a shot; in Picture B, she is giving him some medicine.
3. At the desk in Picture A, the male nurse is standing and holding a clipboard and the female nurse is working at the computer; in Picture B, their roles are reversed.
4. In Picture A, the boy at the desk has his arm in a sling; in Picture B, he is holding his hand to show that it is hurting.
5. In Picture A, the boy at the desk is with his mother (a woman); in Picture B, he is with his father (a man).
6. In Picture A, the little girl in the waiting area at the front has a bandage on her knee (her knee is sprained); in Picture B, the little girl has a bandage on her ankle and she is resting it on a chair.
7. In Picture A, the man in the waiting area has a bandage on his arm; in Picture B, the man is holding a handkerchief to his nose; he has a bloody nose.
8. In Picture A, the man in the wheelchair is reading a newspaper; in Picture B, he is sleeping.

ADJUSTING THE LEVEL

Down: Before students do the activity, have Student As and Students Bs work in separate groups and describe the picture that they have. Have them try to locate each item on the list in the box. You may want to introduce this additional vocabulary: *screen, waiting room, desk, examining table, clipboard.*

   Then have students, in their groups, describe each part of the picture. Prompt with questions such as the following, which you can write on the board:
   • Who is at the left behind the screen?
   • Who is in the waiting area?
   • Which people have medical problems? Where are they? What's wrong with each person?
   • What is the doctor behind the screen doing?
   • What is the nurse behind the screen doing?

Up: Have pairs make a word web with all the medical terms that relate to the pictures. Suggest that students use these categories in their web (the categories go into large circles; the related words can go on lines outside the circle):
   • People and medicine (e.g., doctor, nurse, patient)
   • Illnesses (e.g., sprain, broken bone)
   • Tools (e.g., x-ray, bandage, shot)
   • Things to help patients (e.g., medicine, shot)
Have pairs compare their completed webs.

PROJECT   APPENDIX 2

Health Insurance

1	GROUP	SURVEY	▲

Language Focus: Discussing health insurance, using interview skills
Time: 10 minutes (In addition, students do fieldwork outside of class.)

ADJUSTING THE LEVEL
Up: Have students discuss one or more of the following topics in small groups and report the results to the class:
   • the advantages and disadvantages of national health insurance
   • the advantages and disadvantages of the health insurance system in their countries (or the country where they currently live)
   • a fair cost for private health insurance
   • the most important features of a health insurance policy (low cost, choice of doctors, complete emergency coverage, etc.)

E P I S O D E
27
BAD NEWS

THEME Feeling Guilty

| 1 | PARTNER | INTERVIEW |

Language Focus: Giving opinions, talking about personal experiences
Time: 10 minutes

ADJUSTING THE LEVEL
Down: Before students do the activity, discuss the situations shown in the pictures in the activity. Have volunteers tell if they have been in similar situations and if they have felt guilty — that is, if they felt that they had done something wrong and felt sorry about it. As a class, come up with additional situations where people often feel guilty (e.g., you break a promise, you criticize someone and hurt the person's feelings).

Up: After students do the activity, have pairs join together and expand on their answers, talking about a particular experience when they felt guilty about something.

| 2 | GROUP | SURVEY |

Language Focus: Talking about hypothetical situations, interviewing
Time: 15 minutes

ADJUSTING THE LEVEL
Up: After groups do the activity, have students tell the class the reasons for their opinions. Make a class list on the board.

THEME Living Together

| 3 | PARTNER | DISCUSSION |

Language Focus: Talking about everyday activities, negotiating
Classroom Tip: Have pairs share results with the class in order to find out the most common choices.
Time: 10-15 minutes

ADJUSTING THE LEVEL
Up: Before students read the activity, list the six situations on the board. Have students tell what they think is the best ("ideal") solution for sharing the chores or items.

After students do the activity, have them check to see how different their actual answers are from what they thought were ideal solutions. As they do Part B, have pairs discuss any differences between the "ideal solution" and what they decided on.

| 4 | PARTNER | DISCUSSION |

Language Focus: Using vocabulary for household items, negotiating
Classroom Tip: Have pairs share results with the class, and find out the most common choices.
Time: 10-15 minutes

ADJUSTING THE LEVEL
Up: Have pairs produce a list of the eight items of furniture and a floor plan to show how they would arrange them.

| 5 | PARTNER | ROLE-PLAY |

Language Focus: Discussing preferences, using language related to art
Time: 15-20 minutes

ADJUSTING THE LEVEL
Down: Before students do the activity, go over the expressions from page 2 of Episode 18, Appreciating Art.
- It makes me feel (happy, upset, nervous).
- I like/don't like it.
- It's very (beautiful, funny, ugly).
- It bothers me.
- It relaxes me.
You might also want to add:
- It's too modern/old-fashioned.
- It's too abstract/sentimental.
- It doesn't fit in with _____.

THEME Lying

| 6 | PARTNER | OPINION SURVEY |

Language Focus: Giving opinions
Classroom Tip: Have pairs share results with the class, and find out the most common choices.
Time: 10 minutes

ADJUSTING THE LEVEL
Up: Have pairs discuss reasons for their answers as they do the activity. Have them compare their answers and reasons with another pair.

Then have a class discussion. Go over each item and have volunteers tell why they agree or disagree with it.

Finally, ask volunteers to tell about an experience with a lie. It can be a lie that they told or a lie that someone else told them.

| 7 | GROUP | GAME | ⬍ |

Language Focus: Describing people and events
Time: 15-20 minutes

ADJUSTING THE LEVEL
Down: Have groups work together to write their statements about the character.

Up: Have groups write six statements for their characters and read two at a time, not just one.

GAME Packing for a Quick Trip

| 8 | GROUP | GAME | ⬍ |

Language Focus: Using vocabulary for items that one takes on a trip, asking yes/no questions
Time: 20 minutes (Students can play the game several times in the course of the episode.)

ADJUSTING THE LEVEL
Down: You may want to provide students with picture dictionaries to help them generate ideas for items.

Have them prepare some questions to ask the other team after they have written their lists. Suggest that they use the list of items from their brainstorming as a guide for formulating questions — but they should be careful not to give their own items away!
    EXAMPLE
    •Do you have anything for taking care of your hair?
     (could be hairbrush, comb, or shampoo)
    •Do you have anything for your entertainment?
     (could be a book, music, and so on)

Up: After students play the game, have individual students write on a piece of paper the ten items that they would take with them. Below that have them list the ten items that they think will be the most common choices of the class.

Collect the papers and find the ten most popular items (from the first list on students' papers). Then find the winner (the student whose second list matched the ten most popular items most closely).

Religion and Faith

| 1 | GROUP | RESEARCH | ▼ |

Language Focus: Using sources to get information, talking about religion, making oral presentations, making comparisons
Time: 20-30 minutes (In addition, students do research outside of class.)

ADJUSTING THE LEVEL
Down: First, have students find the meaning of the following words in dictionaries and discuss them: *pray, worship, forgive, sins, morals/morality, monastery/monk, sacrifice, suffering, nirvana, heaven.*

Then model doing the activity for one of the religions. Show students an article from an encyclopedia on an overhead and help them find the information in the article to answer the questions.

| 2 | GROUP | DISCUSSION | ▼ |

Language Focus: Writing a definition, making comparisons
Time: 15 minutes

ADJUSTING THE LEVEL
Down: To guide students' thinking, write down the following list of vocabulary that they can use in the definitions: *belief/believe, God/gods, eternal life, morality.*

E P I S O D E
28
BROTHERS

THEME Worrying

| 1 | PARTNER | INTERVIEW | ▲ |

Language Focus: Talking about personal experiences, interviewing
Time: 5-10 minutes

ADJUSTING THE LEVEL

Up: Have pairs discuss the reasons for their worries and more specifically what it is they worry about. Have partners give advice to help.

> **EXAMPLE**
> A: I worry about school. I need to get good grades. I want to get into a good college/graduate school.
> B: You're a good student. You shouldn't worry so much.

| 2 | GROUP | DISCUSSION | ▲ |

Language Focus: Making generalizations
Time: 10-15 minutes

ADJUSTING THE LEVEL

Up: Before the groups get together, have pairs predict the four most common worries. Ask them to write the worries down on a piece of paper, and hand the paper in to you.

After the activity is completed, identify the pairs whose guesses were the closest.

| 3 | PARTNER | WORRYING TEST | ▼▲ |

Language Focus: Talking about one's personal experiences, interviewing
Time: 10-15 minutes

ADJUSTING THE LEVEL

Down: Before students do the activity, have them describe what is happening in the pictures at the top of the activity. Have students complete these sentence frames:

> She is worrying about _____ing _____.
> She is worrying about how _____.

Help them complete the sentences.

> **EXAMPLE**
> •She is worrying about failing English.
> •She is worrying about having enough money to pay the rent.
> •She is worrying about how she looks.

After students do the activity, have one student from each pair tell another pair what his/her partner worries about.

Up: Have pairs write a letter of advice to the woman in the pictures. She has scored 16 points on the Worrying Test! What does she need to do?

THEME Forgiving

| 4 | GROUP | DISCUSSION | ▼▲ |

Language Focus: Giving opinions
Classroom Tip: Have groups compare their rankings.
Time: 15-20 minutes

ADJUSTING THE LEVEL

Down: Model going through some of the items and ranking them. Elaborate on the nature of the situations and the reasons for your decisions.

> **EXAMPLE**
> Situation A
> This isn't very serious. I was angry and my friend was angry. We were both wrong to be angry. So I'll forgive my friend, and I'll say I'm sorry too.

Up: Have students come up with a solution for each of the problems, using the format described in Part B.

| 5 | PARTNER | WAYS TO SAY IT | ▼▲ |

Language Focus: Apologizing and forgiving
Time: 10 minutes

ADJUSTING THE LEVEL

Down: Help students with the language for apologizing. Write the following sentence frames on the board:

> I apologize for _____ ing.
> I am sorry for _____ ing.
> I am sorry that _____.

As a class, formulate two or three ways of apologizing for each of the following situations:
1. You are late for an appointment.
2. You forgot to tell your friend about a homework assignment.
3. You lost a book your friend lent you.

Answers for Situation 1 above:
• I apologize for being late.
• I am sorry for being late.
• I am sorry that I am late.

Up: Have pairs choose two of the situations in Activity 5 and prepare a role-play of at least four exchanges where one person apologizes to the other. Have pairs share their role-plays in groups.

Then have pairs choose one of the situations from Activity 4 and make up a role-play to present to the class.

6 | PARTNER | PUZZLE ▼

Language Focus: Problem solving
Time: 5-10 minutes
Answer Key: Kevin has one quarter, three dimes, and four nickels. He has enough change to buy the cold drink. He has 75¢.

ADJUSTING THE LEVEL

Down:
Have students work with actual change — let each set of partners use a variety of quarters, dimes, and nickels and suggest that they try different combinations of coins in order to solve the puzzle. (Hint: each group should have at least two quarters, five dimes, and six nickels.)

Another option is to do the puzzle as a class. Set up a chart like the one below. This provides a visual aid in mapping out the possibilities for coins.

quarters	dimes	nickels	
1 quarter = 25¢	1 dime = 10¢	1 nickel = 5¢	
the number of quarters + 3 = the number of nickels	there are two more dimes than quarters	the number of quarters + 3 = the number of nickels	
x	x + 2	x + 3	= 8 coins
1 quarter = 25¢	3 dimes = 30¢	4 nickels =20¢	total= 75¢

INFORMATION GAP **Reunions**

7 | PARTNER | INFORMATION GAP ↕

Language Focus: Talking about oneself, asking for and giving information
Time: 15-20 minutes

ADJUSTING THE LEVEL

Down: Before students do the activity, have Student As and Student Bs work in separate groups. Student As read the paragraph in Part Two on their page and find the following information:
- Where you live
- Your job
- Your marital status
- When you last saw Rebecca

Student Bs find the same information by looking at the paragraph in Part One on their page.

Up: Have students act out similar role-plays about themselves. They are meeting someone that they haven't seen in years. The person asks them questions like those in the activity. Each student should have a turn at being interviewed.

Obituaries

1 | PARTNER | RESEARCH ▼

Language Focus: Reading English-language sources, making generalizations
Classroom Tip: Talk about the kinds of information in Mr. Casey's obituary, pictured on the page. Also, have available obituaries for two or three famous people who died recently.
Time: 5-10 minutes (In addition, students do research outside of class.)

ADJUSTING THE LEVEL

Down: It is recommended that you do this activity as a class. Have two or three obituaries on overheads and help students identify and code common categories of information (e.g., birth place and date, marital status, number of children/grandchildren, early career, accomplishments).

2 | PARTNER | PRESENTATION ↕

Language Focus: Reading English-language sources, describing people, summarizing information, making presentations, giving opinions
Time: 20-30 minutes (In addition, students do research outside of class.)

ADJUSTING THE LEVEL

Down: Have pairs give their presentation to you before they give it to the class. They may show you the obituary and you can help them locate and summarize the information necessary to answer the questions in the activity.

Up: Have students try to find the information for as many of the categories listed in Activity 1, Part B, as they can.

EPISODE
29

GRIEF

THEME Memories

[1] GROUP — DISCUSSION ▼

Language Focus: Talking about personal experiences
Time: 15-20 minutes

ADJUSTING THE LEVEL
Down: Before students write their answers, talk about a few of your first memories (from the list in the activity). With the class, write brief descriptions of your memories on the board. Then have volunteers share some of their memories, and write brief descriptions of these on the board.

[2] CLASS — MEMORY BINGO ↕

Language Focus: Talking about personal experiences
Classroom Tip: As an extra activity, have students share some of their memories from the items on the bingo board.
Time: 15-25 minutes

ADJUSTING THE LEVEL
Down: Before students do the activity, go through some of the squares and have students give a memory related to it. Where necessary, prompt by giving some of your own memories.

Up: After playing bingo, have students choose two of the squares and write a paragraph about a memorable experience for each. Ask students to put each paragraph on a separate piece of paper and write their names on their papers. Post the paragraphs. Encourage class members to read the paragraphs and write comments and reactions, such as whether they have had similar experiences and whether they think the paragraphs are humorous.

THEME Pipe Dreams

[3] PARTNER — INTERVIEW ▲

Language Focus: Talking about personal dreams and plans, interviewing
Time: 5-10 minutes

ADJUSTING THE LEVEL
Up: Have students interview their partners about one of their dreams. For example, *What special talent would you like to have? Why do you want that talent?* Have students tell what they learn about their partner to another pair.

[4] PARTNER — DISCUSSION ▲

Language Focus: Discussing dreams and plans, describing a picture, interviewing
Time: 10-15 minutes

ADJUSTING THE LEVEL
Up: Have students each write a paragraph on their partner's pipe dream based on the information that they have asked for in their discussion. Have each student share the paragraph with his/her partner, who can suggest changes.

[5] GROUP — DISCUSSION ▼

Language Focus: Reading statements and drawing conclusions, talking about dreams and plans
Time: 5-10 minutes
Answer Key: The most likely answers are the following:
- Mrs. Mendoza — "I hope to have a beautiful home in Mexico . . ."
- Alex — "I'd like to be a professional baseball player . . ."
- Ramón — "I want to make this restaurant a big success . . ."
- Matt — "I want to get married soon . . ."
- Alberto — "I want to be a professional photographer . . ."

ADJUSTING THE LEVEL
Down: Before students do the activity, have them recall basic information about the characters in the list and what they like.
> EXAMPLE
> Mrs. Mendoza
> She works in the restaurant. The restaurant is important to her. She likes to dance and sing. Her family is important to her.

THEME Funeral Customs

[6] CLASS — DISCUSSION ↕

Language Focus: Talking about customs/culture
Time: 10-15 minutes

ADJUSTING THE LEVEL
Down: Before students do the activity, ask them to list as a class the funeral customs that they remember from Mr. Casey's funeral in the video. Have them compare their list with the items given in Activity 6.

Up: Have students write a composition in which they compare and contrast funeral customs in the United States with those in their home country. Guide the composition by making the outline:

1. Funerals in the United States and funerals in my country are alike in some ways, but different in some ways, too.

    A) One of the basic ways in which funerals are alike is that in both countries, . . . Also, . . .
    [Paragraph discusses *similarities*]

B) One of the basic ways in which funerals are different is that (in my country) . . .
[Paragraph discusses *differences*]

Model writing the composition, based on information from a volunteer.

GAME Expressing Emotions

| 7 | GROUP | GAME | ⬍ |

Language Focus: Using vocabulary for emotions, discussing personal experiences
Time: 15-20 minutes (Students can play the game several times in the course of the episode.)

ADJUSTING THE LEVEL

Down: Before students do the activity, review the vocabulary of emotions. Have students look in dictionaries to find the meaning of any word about which they are unsure. Then have the students illustrate the meaning of the emotions in the activity by acting them. On the board, with the class, make a list of emotions and situations in which people might experience them.

EXAMPLE
nervous:
• You have a job interview.
• You have a big test.

disappointed:
• You get a bad grade on your composition.
• You invited someone to come to a party, but he/she can't come.

Then have students discuss their personal experiences with emotions.

EXAMPLE
• It makes me feel embarrassed when I have to speak in class.
• When I am nervous, I try to relax. I sometimes take deep breaths.

Up: After students play the game, have them work in pairs to role-play a situation in which one of the students expresses one of the emotions from the activity and the other student reacts.

PROJECT   APPENDIX 5

Honoring the Dead

| 1 | PARTNER | RESEARCH | ⬍ |

Language Focus: Discussing/reading about customs/culture, using various sources to get information, using interview skills, summarizing, making comparisons
Time: 5-10 minutes (In addition, students do research outside of class.)

ADJUSTING THE LEVEL

Down: Before students do the activity, invite volunteers to tell about days honoring the dead in their country and what people do on those days. Write a list of activities on the board.

Up: Have students summarize in a paragraph what they find out about each day honoring the dead. Another idea is to have students discuss the customs as a class and come up with a master list of similarities among two or more cultures.

| 2 | GROUP | PRESENTATION | ⬍ |

Language Focus: Using various sources to get information, making a presentation
Time: 20-30 minutes (In addition, students do research outside of class.)

ADJUSTING THE LEVEL

Down: Before students do the activity, have them discuss the memorials pictured and tell what they know about them. (Point out that on the Vietnam Memorial are the names of American soldiers who died in the war.)

Up: Have students take notes as they listen to the presentations. Have each student tell the two most surprising facts he/she learned.

After the presentations, have a class discussion about the similarities and differences among the memorials (such as whom they honor, why they were created).

E P I S O D E
30
LIFE GOES ON

THEME Making Plans for the Future

1 | PARTNER | WAYS TO SAY IT | ⬍

Language Focus: Talking about plans
Time: 5-10 minutes

ADJUSTING THE LEVEL
Down: Go over the expressions in the box. Ask students what they plan to do over the weekend or during the summer.

Then ask each student to say what he/she plans to do when he/she has some free time. Follow up by asking what other students remember about their classmates' answers: *What does _____ plan to do when he/she has some free time?*

Up: Have students work in groups. One of them is an interviewer for a TV station, doing person-in-the-street interviews. The two questions for the day are these:
• What big items do you plan to do buy this year?
• What will you do for vacation this year?

2 | PARTNER | SURVEY | ▲

Language Focus: Giving personal information, interviewing
Time: 10 minutes

ADJUSTING THE LEVEL
Up: With the class, brainstorm a list of common plans for each of these items.

> EXAMPLE
> *making/saving money:* save a certain percentage of one's income, buy stock, make investments
> *retirement:* have a retirement plan/pension, buy a retirement house on the beach

3 | PARTNER | WRITING | ▼

Language Focus: Talking about plans, interviewing
Time: 20-30 minutes

ADJUSTING THE LEVEL
Down: Before students do the activity, model it by having students ask you the questions. Volunteers can write your answers on the board. Then, as a class, write a paragraph.

THEME Neighbors

4 | PARTNER | GOOD NEIGHBOR TEST | ⬍

Language Focus: Talking about personal experiences, interviewing
Time: 5-10 minutes

ADJUSTING THE LEVEL
Down: Have the class ask you and several volunteers the questions. Make the context of the questions clear by your answers (e.g., mention what you lent your neighbor, or what favor you did).

Up: Have pairs come up with a list of at least five things that a good neighbor does. Ask pairs to share their lists. Then come up with a master class list, which you write on the board.

Another activity is to have students give reasons for each of the following statements:
• It is good to be friendly with your neighbors.
• It is not good to be friendly with your neighbors.
Take a class vote to find out which statement most students agree with.

5 | GROUP | DISCUSSION | ▼

Language Focus: Discussing problems and solutions
Time: 15 minutes

ADJUSTING THE LEVEL
Down: If necessary, prompt students with ideas such as the following: problems with noise, problems with animals, problems with parking, problems with fences. Also, provide students with sentence frames to help them construct their solutions, such as the following:
> I would _____.
> We could _____.
> It's a good idea to _____.

THEME Following Parents' Wishes

6 | GROUP | DISCUSSION | ▼

Language Focus: Talking about personal experiences, talking about wishes/plans, interviewing
Time: 10 minutes

ADJUSTING THE LEVEL
Down: Before students do the activity, brainstorm a list of common wishes that parents have for their children.
> EXAMPLE
> •get a good job
> •marry a nice person
> •have a special talent
> •be happy
> •have a nice house

7 | GROUP | DISCUSSION | ▲

Language Focus: Discussing everyday situations, giving opinions
Classroom Tip: After the activity is finished, have groups report results and add up the votes to find overall results for the class for each situation.
Time: 5-10 minutes

ADJUSTING THE LEVEL
Up: After groups make their choices, go over each situation and have the groups tell why they made the choices they did. Write the most common reasons on the board.

INFORMATION GAP Family Traits

8 | PARTNER | INFORMATION GAP | ♦

Language Focus: Reading a description of people, making generalizations, asking for and giving information
Time: 15-20 minutes
Answer Key: Picture A: from left to right, Hiromi, Yoko, Michiko, Motoi, Toshi; possible answer for ways they are alike: most of the family members like music and work in music-related jobs. *Picture B:* from left to right, Marta, Lupe, Bob, Ricardo, Luis; possible answer for ways they are alike: most of the family members work with children as teachers.

ADJUSTING THE LEVEL
Down: Before students do the activity, have Student As and Student Bs work in separate groups. First, have them talk about the picture on the page. (Student As work on page 5, and Student Bs work on page 6.) Tell them to try to answer these questions:
* Who is the youngest?
* Who is the tallest?
* Who is the oldest?

Then have them read over the paragraph in the box. Have them write down information about each person in a chart form. They can use their charts during the activity.

    EXAMPLE
    Student A

Lupe   38, oldest of sisters and brothers, housewife/ works in a day care center

Luis   teaches sports to children

Up: After students do the activity, have them tell their partners about each of the people in the picture on their page, using the information that they remember from the activity.

Making Donations

1 | GROUP | RESEARCH | ♦

Language Focus: Using various sources to get information, using interview skills, talking about social organizations, talking about customs/culture
Classroom Tip: You may want to have a list of local charities available to share with students. Or you might have available in the classroom sources like those listed in the activity to help students find the names of charities.
Time: 5-10 minutes (In addition, students do fieldwork outside of class.)

ADJUSTING THE LEVEL
Down: You may want to give students a list of local charities to investigate. In addition, you might want to have a representative from a local charity talk to the class about the donations it takes and how it uses them.

Up: Have students find out how the charities use donations and about the possibility of doing volunteer work for them.

2 | GROUP | SURVEY | ♦

Language Focus: Using interview skills, talking about customs/culture
Time: 10-15 minutes (In addition, students do fieldwork outside of class.)

ADJUSTING THE LEVEL
Down: Have students prepare for the activity by asking you and several members of the class the questions. In this way, students become familiar with the questions and with language related to charities.

Up: After students do the activity and share results, have each group write an article for a school newspaper about common local charities and how people can donate to them. In their articles, the groups should include addresses and phone numbers of the charities.

E P I S O D E
31
A BOX OF MEMORIES

THEME Spending Money

| 1 | PARTNER | DISCUSSION | ▪ ▲ |

Language Focus: Talking about ways to spend money
Classroom Tip: Have pairs report their choices to the class and determine any items that appear on all lists.
Time: 10-15 minutes

ADJUSTING THE LEVEL
Up: In addition to ranking the items, have students write why they chose the item they did.
> EXAMPLE
> *pay bills:* It is best to be free of debt before you spend more money.
> *pay school tuition:* Going to school is important, and it can even help you make more money in the future.

| 2 | PARTNER | PIE CHART | ⇕ |

Language Focus: Discussing spending money, using math terms
Classroom Tip: If possible, have students make their pie charts on a computer. If not, you may suggest that they trace around a circular object such as a cup bottom in order to make their charts.
Time: 20-30 minutes

ADJUSTING THE LEVEL
Down: Provide students with useful language for Part C:
> *comparing charts*
> We are spending more money on ____.
> We are spending less money on ____.
> We are spending most of our money on ____.
> *giving reasons*
> This will help me get more money in the future.
> It is important to have a (house/car).
> It is important to enjoy oneself.

Up: As a follow-up, have pairs make up a chart for Kevin and Rebecca. Have pairs compare charts and give reasons for their choices.

THEME Mementos

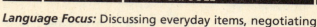

| 3 | GROUP | SURVEY | ▼ |

Language Focus: Describing personal experiences
Time: 15 minutes

ADJUSTING THE LEVEL
Down: Lead a discussion of mementos.
1. Have students discuss the mementos that Mr. Casey had in his safety deposit box: a ring, old photographs, a program from a school event his daughter was in, and so on.
2. Discuss any mementos you have and ask volunteers to talk about theirs.

| 4 | GROUP | TIME CAPSULE | ⇕ |

Language Focus: Discussing everyday items, negotiating
Time: 20-30 minutes

ADJUSTING THE LEVEL
Down: Before students do the activity, have them brainstorm lists of things that are symbols/part of their everyday lives. Make a master list on the board. The groups can use this as the basis for preparing their lists.

Up: Have students in each group write a paragraph about the school they are attending for inclusion in the time capsule. They should describe what classes are like, what the typical student is like, and what the typical teacher is like.

| 5 | CLASS | GAME | ▼ |

Language Focus: Describing people and items associated with them
Time: 15-20 minutes

ADJUSTING THE LEVEL
Down: To model the activity, ask the class to think of two famous people and brainstorm three items associated with each person. Suggest that they think of movie stars, sports figures, politicians, musicians, writers, and so on. Write the answers on the board.

As pairs write their lists to complete the activity, circulate around the class and provide help with ideas and with spelling.

THEME Being Independent

| 6 | GROUP | SURVEY | |

Language Focus: Discussing personal characteristics, giving opinions
Time: 10-15 minutes

ADJUSTING THE LEVEL
Down: Before students do the activity, have the class come up with a list of things that a person needs to be independent.

EXAMPLE
- a job
- one's own apartment
- savings
- ability to do household chores
- ability to organize one's finances and budget

Up: As students ask the question, have them also ask the following question: *Why do you think that is important?* Have them note the answers.

| 7 | PARTNER | DATA ANALYSIS | ▲ |

Language Focus: Making generalizations
Classroom Tip: Have pairs report on the most common answer/answers from each column. Have the students try to make generalizations about the things most class members think a person needs to be independent.
Time: 10-15 minutes

ADJUSTING THE LEVEL
Up: Have two pairs work together and write a report of their findings. They should try to answer these questions:
1. What items do most people agree are important? (These are in the middle column.)
2. Do you have more items in the left and right columns or in the middle column?
3. Look at your answer to question 2 above. Do women and men agree or disagree on what is important for independence?
4. Look at your answer to question 3 above. If men and women disagree, how can you explain the differences?

GAME Family Jewelry

| 8 | GROUP | GAME | ▲▼ |

Language Focus: Using vocabulary for jewelry, relatives, and rooms in a house
Time: 15 minutes (Students can play the game several times in the course of the episode.)

ADJUSTING THE LEVEL
Down: Review the vocabulary needed to do the activity, particularly the items in the box at the top of the page. Then play a guessing game. Give clues to meaning and have students raise their hands when they know the word.

> EXAMPLE
> - People wear these on their hands.
> - People wear these in their ears.
> - A room with a lot of books.
> - Your father's sister.

Put the game board on an overhead projector and demonstrate how to play the game with a couple of volunteers.

Up: After a few rounds, have students make their own sets of game cards with additional pieces of jewelry and relatives.

PROJECT   APPENDIX 7

Ellis Island

| 1 | GROUP | RESEARCH | ▼ |

Language Focus: Using English-language sources to get information, answering questions about history, making oral presentations
Classroom Tip: Have available books on Ellis Island, preferably those written at a simple language level, appropriate for students learning English.
Time: 15 minutes (In addition, students do research outside of class.)

ADJUSTING THE LEVEL
Down: If the task is very difficult for students, provide them with sources and indicate the sections/paragraphs where they can find answers. Meet with each group as it is preparing its answers.

EPISODE 32

THE MISSING CAR

THEME **Treating**

| 1 | GROUP | DISCUSSION | ⬍ |

Language Focus: Discussing customs/culture
Classroom Tip: After the activity is finished, have groups report results and add up the votes to find overall results for the class for each item.
Time: 10 minutes

ADJUSTING THE LEVEL

Down: Before students do the activity, discuss the situation in each picture with the class.

After students do the activity, ask which of the choices would be most common in their countries for the item. Have students raise their hand for each choice/item and take a tally.

Explain that in the United States these are probably the most common choices:

1. Choice 1 or 3: The man should treat or both should pay.
2. Choice 2: The boss should treat.
3. Choice 3: Everyone should pay.
4. Choice 1: The businessperson should treat.

Up: Explain the common choices for the United States listed above. Have students write paragraphs in which they tell how customs in their countries are the same or different.

THEME **Likes and Dislikes**

| 2 | PARTNER | WAYS TO SAY IT | ⬍ |

Language Focus: Expressing likes and dislikes
Classroom Tip: Explain that *I adore* and *I am wild* are used in informal speech with friends rather than in formal settings such as a classroom. They both indicate a high degree of liking. The phrases *I hate* and *I detest* indicate a high degree of dislike.
Time: 10-15 minutes

ADJUSTING THE LEVEL

Down: Help students generate a list of categories for each item:

> EXAMPLE
> *restaurants:* French, Italian; fast-food, elegant; self-service versus having a waiter/waitress

> *sports:* soccer, baseball, football, jogging; team sports versus individual sports; being a spectator versus being a participant
> *movies:* comedies, dramas, action movies, Westerns; American, French, Japanese; long versus short
> *music:* jazz, blues, rock and roll

Write the sentence frames on the board so that students understand how to make sentences with *would rather* and *prefer*.

> I'd rather _____ than _____.
> I'd rather stay home than go out.
> I prefer _____ to _____.
> I prefer shrimp to oysters.

Up: Tell pairs to discuss their likes and dislikes until they find:

- one item they both like in each category
- one item they both dislike in each category
- one item one likes and the other doesn't like in each category

Have each student write down sentences describing himself/herself and his/her partner. Then ask students to share their sentences with a different pair.

> EXAMPLE
> Ed adores horror films, but I detest them.

| 3 | GROUP | PRESENTATION | ⬍ |

Language Focus: Expressing likes and dislikes
Classroom Tip: You may want to coordinate the activity so that each group gives different awards and there is no overlap. Also, you may want students (or a committee) to design a class award. Enough of these awards can then be made for each group to hand out its four awards.
Time: 20-30 minutes

ADJUSTING THE LEVEL

Down: With the class, brainstorm additional awards, as well as recipients for the awards.

Up: Have groups prepare a short speech of about a minute for each of its four awards, explaining why they chose the award and the recipient. Different group members should give each of the four speeches.

| 4 | CLASS | STORYTELLING | ⬇ |

Language Focus: Summarizing stories
Time: 20 minutes

ADJUSTING THE LEVEL

Down: Have students work in pairs and discuss their lists as they prepare them.

Help students summarize stories. Put these questions on the board and tell students to try to answer them:

- Where does the story take place?
- Who are the main characters in the story?
- What is the problem in the story?
- How do the characters try to solve the problem?

THEME **Seafood**

5 | TEAM | GAME ⬍

Language Focus: Using vocabulary for seafood
Classroom Tip: Have encyclopedias, dictionaries, or picture dictionaries available for students to refer to as they do the activity.
Time: 10 minutes
Answer Key: Fish: perch, swordfish, salmon, catfish, rainbow trout, eel; *Shellfish:* oyster, lobster, clam, scallop, crab

ADJUSTING THE LEVEL

Down: Tell students to use dictionaries or encyclopedias as they do the activity (these typically list categories for each type of fish).

Up: Tell students to add as many fish to each category as they can. Teams get one point for each fish.

6 | PARTNER | INTERVIEW ⬆

Language Focus: Talking about food, talking about personal preferences and experiences
Time: 10 minutes

ADJUSTING THE LEVEL

Up: After students do the activity, have each student write a paragraph about his/her food experiences related to fish. Students can try to answer these questions:
• Which fish dishes do you commonly eat?
• How often do you eat fish?
• Which fish do you really dislike?
• Which fish dishes do you like best?
• What was the best fish meal you have ever eaten?

INFORMATION GAP **Restaurants**

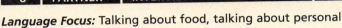

7 | PARTNER | INFORMATION GAP ⬍

Language Focus: Using vocabulary for foods and restaurants, asking for and giving information
Classroom Tip: You might want to model how to read U.S. addresses: they are typically read as two sets of two numbers. For example, 1987 South Street is read *nineteen eighty-seven;* 234 East Avenue is read *two thirty-four.*
Time: 15 minutes

ADJUSTING THE LEVEL

Down: Have Student As and Student Bs work in separate groups. (Student As look at page 5; Student Bs look at page 6.) For each restaurant in the listings, have them underline the following:
• the kind of restaurant
• types of food you can eat there
• the price range

Up: Have students use actual restaurant listings for a local area or a U.S. city and try to find the types of restaurants asked for in the activity.

PROJECT   APPENDIX 8

Symbols and Symbolism

1 | PARTNER | RESEARCH ⬇

Language Focus: Using various sources to get information, making an oral presentation
Classroom Tip: Assign different groups different topics according to students' interests.
Time: 20-30 minutes (In addition, students do research outside of class.)

ADJUSTING THE LEVEL

Down: Make available to students sources that discuss some of these items. (Encyclopedias and almanacs would work well.) Students can use them as the basis for their research.

2 | GROUP | FIELDWORK ⬍

Language Focus: Describing everyday items, giving personal reactions
Classroom Tip: Make a master list of symbols found on the board.
Time: 15 minutes (In addition, students do fieldwork outside of class.)

ADJUSTING THE LEVEL

Down: Before students do the activity, discuss and describe a few common symbols as a class

Up: Encourage students to include in their lists where they saw each symbol, its description, and its meaning. Invite volunteers to draw common symbols on the board.

E P I S O D E

33

A BREAKDOWN

THEME Favorite Places

| 1 | PARTNER | INTERVIEW | ▲▼ |

Language Focus: Talking about personal experiences, describing places
Time: 10 minutes

ADJUSTING THE LEVEL
Down: Before students do the activity, have them discuss and describe Kevin's favorite place. Ask: *Why do you think it is his favorite place?* Ask volunteers to share any favorite places. Help them describe the places and tell why they like them.

Up: Have students write about one of their favorite places, describing it in detail and telling why it is a favorite. Have students share their paragraphs with their partners.

| 2 | PARTNER | PUZZLE | ▲▼ |

Language Focus: Understanding location words
Time: 10 minutes
Answer Key: Top row, from left to right: Gino's Pizza, Bake Shop, fire station, park, music store; *Bottom row, from left to right:* Today's Hair Salon, public library, Sweetheart's Ice Cream Parlor, Kelley's Florist, Rita's Coffee Shop

ADJUSTING THE LEVEL
Down: Before students do the activity, review the key location words by describing the locations of stores and other places in your area. You might draw a simple outline map on the board or have local maps available. Write the following phrases on the board for students to use in their descriptions of locations: *next to, across from, opposite, between, on the same street as.*
Prompt with questions such as these:
• Where's the school?
• Where's the hospital?

Up: Have students play a follow-up game in pairs. Give them five minutes to describe the places on the map in as many ways as they can. The pair with the most correct answers wins.

  EXAMPLE
  •The fire station is between the Bake Shop and the park.
  •The fire station is on the same street as the music store.
  •The fire station is opposite the public library.

THEME Keeping in Touch

| 3 | CLASS | SURVEY | ▲ |

Language Focus: Talking about personal experiences, using vocabulary for ways to communicate
Time: 5-10 minutes

ADJUSTING THE LEVEL
Up: After the class does the activity, have them work in groups and write down the advantages and disadvantages of each kind of communication.

  EXAMPLE
  calling people long-distance on the telephone

  Advantages:
  •You have immediate contact with the person.
  •It's fast and easy.

  Disadvantages:
  •It can cost a lot of money to call long-distance.
Then have the groups share their lists. The class can vote on the best way to keep in touch with people far away.

| 4 | CLASS | DISCUSSION | ▲ |

Language Focus: Talking about personal experiences
Classroom Tip: Find the students with the highest numbers and write their names and answers on the board.
Time: 10-15 minutes

ADJUSTING THE LEVEL
Up: After the discussion, have students work in small groups to compare their answers with those of their classmates.
  EXAMPLE
  I made about eight phone calls to friends and family far away. This is only one third as many as the highest number — 24.

THEME Anger

| 5 | PARTNER | INTERVIEW | ▲ |

Language Focus: Talking about personal experiences, interviewing
Time: 10 minutes

ADJUSTING THE LEVEL
Up: Have pairs compare answers. Then ask them to discuss these questions:
  • What are good ways to handle anger?
  • What are bad ways to handle anger?

| 6 | PARTNER | DISCUSSION | ▲▼ |

Language Focus: Giving opinions
Classroom Tip: Have pairs report results and find the four most common things that make students in the class angry.
Time: 10-15 minutes

ADJUSTING THE LEVEL

Down: Before students do the activity, discuss two or three things that make you angry, such as when people cut in front of you in line, when you have to wait a long time to get food in a restaurant, when students come late to class. Have students tell if any of those things make them angry too.

Up: Have students describe their partner's answers to another pair.

GAME Lost and Found

7	PARTNER	GAME	⬍

Language Focus: Spelling English words
Classroom Tip: Make additional grids so that students can play the game several times.
Time: 10-15 minutes (The students can play additional games if you provide pieces of graph paper to make more grids.)

ADJUSTING THE LEVEL

Down: Demonstrate how to play the game. Make a sample grid on the board or on an overhead with several words. Have volunteers be "guessers"; they guess locations such as *A5* or *F6*. You give responses such as *That's a hit.* and *You're getting warm.*

Up: Have students play the game again, this time using other words from the *Connect with English* series. You will need to provide students with additional grids.

Adulthood

1	GROUP	RESEARCH	⬍

Language Focus: Using various sources to get information, using interview skills, discussing laws/customs
Time: 10 minutes (In addition, students do research outside of class.)

ADJUSTING THE LEVEL

Down: Before students do the activity, have them make guesses about whether there is a minimum age for each category and, if so, what the age might be. This can be done as a class.

Up: Suggest that students first ask people and then get information from official government offices or documents. Then they can determine if people seem to know the right information about the laws.

2	GROUP	DISCUSSION	⬇

Language Focus: Giving opinions
Time: 15 minutes

ADJUSTING THE LEVEL

Down: Present students with some useful language for giving their opinions about minimum age. Write sentence frames such as the following on the board.

EXAMPLE
I would change the law about _____.
I think that _____ is too low an age.
I think that _____ year-olds are old enough to be responsible for their actions.
I don't think that _____ year-olds are old enough to make that decision.

EPISODE
34
A CALL FOR HELP

THEME **Confrontations**

1 | GROUP | SURVEY | ▲

Language Focus: Giving opinions, interviewing
Time: 10-15 minutes

ADJUSTING THE LEVEL

Up: After groups do the survey, have them analyze the results by discussing these questions:
- Are there any differences between when students would confront a stranger and when they would confront a friend? Will students confront a stranger in situations where they wouldn't confront a friend?
- Are there some students who do not like to confront others? For example, are there some students who answered no to all or most of the questions?

THEME **Making Compromises**

2 | PARTNER | DISCUSSION | ▼

Language Focus: Talking about everyday situations, making compromises
Time: 10-15 minutes

ADJUSTING THE LEVEL

Down: Before students do the activity, have them identify the compromise shown in the pictures. Then, as a class, have students brainstorm compromises to the following situations:
1. A: You want to decorate your apartment in a modern style.
   B: You want to decorate your apartment in a traditional style.
2. A: You want to stay home for the weekend.
   B: You want to go to the beach for the weekend.
3. A: You want to go on vacation in the summer.
   B: You want to go on vacation in the winter.

3 | PARTNER | ROLE-PLAY | ▼

Language Focus: Making compromises, making suggestions
Time: 20-30 minutes

ADJUSTING THE LEVEL

Down: Review some of the language for making suggestions and compromises. Write the following on the board:
- *Making a suggestion:* Let's go _____. / Why don't we _____?
- *Saying no to a suggestion:* Oh, I don't want to _____.
- *Agreeing to a suggestion:* Sounds good to me. / OK. That's a great idea.
- *Offering another idea:* Let's go _____ instead. / I'd rather go _____.

Have students find the expressions in the sample conversation in Activity 2. Then tell students to use the list as they make up their role-plays.

4 | PARTNER | DISCUSSION | ▼

Language Focus: Talking about personal experiences, making generalizations
Time: 15-20 minutes

ADJUSTING THE LEVEL

Down: Before students do the activity, brainstorm a list of common situations where people compromise.
   EXAMPLE
   • Who will do a household chore
   • Where to go for entertainment
   • Where to live
   • How to spend money

Then think of a compromise that you have made. Have students ask you the questions in the box, and have volunteers write your answers on the board.

Ask volunteers to tell of compromises they have made and whether they were easy or hard. Have the class try to categorize the compromise, using categories such as those above, and see whether compromises are easier in some categories than in others.

5 | GROUP | DISCUSSION | ⇕

Language Focus: Giving opinions
Classroom Tip: After students do the activity, have groups share results and come up with a list of top five good ideas for making compromises.
Time: 10-15 minutes

ADJUSTING THE LEVEL

Down: Do this as a class activity first, with volunteers stating their answers and giving examples to support their opinions.

Up: In their discussion, have groups give reasons for their opinions.
   EXAMPLE
   try to see only two solutions to the problem

   This is not a good idea. If you try to think of more solutions, you might find a better one.

THEME   Considering Options

| 6 | TEAM | GAME | ⬍ |

Language Focus: Giving advice/making suggestions
Time: 10 minutes

ADJUSTING THE LEVEL

Down: Have students of lower and higher language proficiency on the same team.

Up: Have individual students write a list of options and then share them with their groups. In this case, add five minutes to the time for the game in order for students to write their lists.

| 7 | GROUP | DISCUSSION | ⬍ |

Language Focus: Giving opinions, giving reasons
Time: 15 minutes

ADJUSTING THE LEVEL

Down: Before students do the activity, choose a few of the options and discuss the advantages and/or disadvantages.

> EXAMPLE
> read the want ads
>
> *Advantage:*
> You can find many jobs.
>
> *Disadvantage:*
> Many people apply for these jobs.

As students work in their groups, have them rank the options listed.

Up: Have students work in pairs and make up a role-play using one of the situations listed in Activity 6. One student gives advice and options to the other. Tell the student giving the advice to choose one good and one not-so-good option. The student getting the advice responds by talking about the advantages or disadvantages of each option.

INFORMATION GAP
Packing and Moving

| 8 | PARTNER | INFORMATION GAP | ⬍ |

Language Focus: Using vocabulary for household items, using location words, asking for and giving information
Time: 15-20 minutes

ADJUSTING THE LEVEL

Down: Before students do the activity, check their comprehension of the furniture vocabulary by giving descriptions and having students guess the item being described.

> EXAMPLE
> You can sit on it. It is bigger than a chair. (sofa)

Then model the activity. Draw an outline of an apartment like those in Activity 8 on the board or on an overhead. Have students tell you where to put the furniture.

> EXAMPLE
> • Put the bookcase on the west wall of the living room.
> • Put the bed on the north wall of the bedroom.
> • Put the dresser under the window in the bedroom.

Up: After students do the activity, have pairs pretend to be interior decorators and come up with the best plan for one of the apartments. In addition to furniture arrangements, they should suggest colors for the rooms and furniture, style of furniture, and types of paintings. Have pairs present their ideas to the class.

PROJECT   APPENDIX 10

Alcohol Abuse

| 1 | GROUP | RESEARCH | ⬇ |

Language Focus: Using various sources to get information, using interview skills
Classroom Tip: Have the names of alcohol abuse programs available, as well as information about them, such as brochures or other literature.
Time: 15-20 minutes (In addition, students do research outside of class.)

ADJUSTING THE LEVEL

Down: Before students do the activity, if possible have a speaker from an alcohol abuse group come to class and answer the questions. As an alternative, show students brochures from alcohol abuse groups and have them find the answers to the questions in the activity.

| 2 | GROUP | RESEARCH | ⬇ |

Language Focus: Using various sources to get information, using interview skills
Classroom Tip: Have groups share the information they find with the class.
Time: 10 minutes (In addition, students do research outside of class.)

ADJUSTING THE LEVEL

Down: Before students do the activity, model it. Try to have a guest from a program come to the class to speak and have students get the answers to the questions. Or get brochures and other literature from a group and help students find the information in the brochure.

EPISODE
35
CHANGES

THEME Best Friends

Language Focus: Giving opinions, discussing ideas about friendship
Time: 15 minutes

ADJUSTING THE LEVEL

Up: After students do the activity, have each member of the group think of one of their best friends. The student is to check the qualities that his/her best friend has. Have students compare their answers in their groups and discuss whether they were surprised by the results.

| 2 | PARTNER | GAME | ◆ |

Language Focus: Discussing personal preferences, interviewing
Classroom Tip: Have students do Part A before they actually look at the page. This way they don't know the actual categories used in the game.
Time: 15-20 minutes

ADJUSTING THE LEVEL

Down: Tell students to take notes as they discuss personal preferences with their partner in Part A. Tell them to talk until each has listed at least ten items about the other.

Up: After pairs do the activity, have each student question his/her partner about two of the answers that he/she found the most interesting or surprising.

THEME Making Threats

| 3 | GROUP | DISCUSSION | ▼ |

Language Focus: Making threats
Time: 10 minutes

ADJUSTING THE LEVEL

Down: Have students discuss ideas as a class first. Encourage them to think about current movies or TV programs to find examples of threats. Make a master list of threats on the board. Then have students discuss threats that you as teacher could make to them (*If you don't study more, I'll give you a quiz every day.*), as well as common threats that parents make to children (*You had better clean your room, or I won't let you watch TV tonight.*).

| 4 | PARTNER | INTERVIEW | ◆ |

Language Focus: Giving opinions, interviewing
Classroom Tip: Explain that the expression *Is that a threat or a promise?* is often used when someone doesn't take a threat seriously.
Time: 5-10 minutes

ADJUSTING THE LEVEL

Down: Have students look at the picture and answer these questions:
1. Who makes the threat?
2. What is the threat?
3. Does the boy take the threat seriously?

Up: Have pairs discuss whether their parents used threats with them or whether they use threats with their children. Have each pair share experiences with another pair. Have pairs judge how effective threats are.

THEME The Family Home

| 5 | PARTNER | ROLE-PLAY | ◆ |

Language Focus: Using vocabulary related to houses, giving descriptions of houses
Time: 15 minutes

ADJUSTING THE LEVEL

Down: Have students look at the pictures and help them describe the "houses":
a. a large modern apartment building
b. a large traditional (Victorian) house (made of wood)
c. a modern single-family home with a lot of glass
d. a small traditional cottage.
   Have the class interview you, using the questions in the activity. Then have pairs write up a description of your "dream" house.

Up: After pairs do the activity, have each "architect" write a description of his/her partner's dream house. Tell students to ask their partner any other questions they want in order to get more details about their partner's dream house.
   EXAMPLE
   • Do you want a fireplace?
   • Do you want a house with a lot of large windows?
   • Do you want a house with a view? What should the view be of? The city? A forest? A lake?
   • Do you want skylights?

Have partners look over the descriptions and make any changes or additions.

| 6 | PARTNER | GAME | ⬍ |

Language Focus: Adding to a story, reading a narrative
Time: 15-20 minutes (Students can play the game several times in the course of the episode.)

ADJUSTING THE LEVEL
Down: Before students do the activity, have them read the squares on the board and have them tell the story of what Smith is doing and what the police officer is doing.

Then, as a class, brainstorm some ideas to use for the Police Officer Cards and the Smith Cards.

Up: Have the pairs play the game. Then each writes a summary of what happened to their character, using the first person.

EXAMPLE
Smith
I had just robbed the museum. I needed to get out of country fast. I didn't want the police to catch me. I didn't want to be arrested!

Support Groups

| 1 | PARTNER | RESEARCH | ▼ |

Language Focus: Using sources to get information, using interview skills
Classroom Tip: Have telephone books available for students to use in the activity.
Time: 10 minutes (In addition, students do fieldwork outside of class. You may want to allow class time for students to find the names of groups.)

ADJUSTING THE LEVEL
Down: Do the activity with students as a class, using a phone book to get as much information as possible.

| 2 | PARTNER | RESEARCH | ▼ |

Language Focus: Using sources to get information, using interview skills, making oral presentations
Time: 20-30 minutes (In addition, students do research/field-work outside of class.)

ADJUSTING THE LEVEL
Down: Before students do the activity, model it. Try to have a guest from a support program come to the class to speak. Have students get the answers to the questions in the activity. As an alternate, model a phone conversation with someone at a community center in which students ask you for information about a support group. (Use information from a support group brochure to provide answers.) This should help students with the phone calls or interviews in their fieldwork, and also help familiarize them with the basic vocabulary.

E P I S O D E
36
THE FARM

THEME City vs. Country

Language Focus: Using vocabulary to describe the city and the country

Classroom Tip: It is best if students have dictionaries available when they do the activity both to check spelling and as a way to find more words.

Time: 15 minutes

ADJUSTING THE LEVEL

Up: In addition to just listing the words, have students use the words in a sentence.

> EXAMPLE
> • <u>Stoplights</u> control traffic.
> • <u>Skyscrapers</u> can hold many offices.
> • The <u>silos</u> hold wheat and grain.
> • <u>Cows</u> often graze in fields.

Students get one point for every word on their lists and one point for every sentence. Tell students that you will be the judge as to whether sentences are acceptable; for example, a sentence such as *A cow is an animal.* is not acceptable because it is too general.

| 2 | CLASS | DEBATE | ⇕ |

Language Focus: Giving reasons
Time: 20 minutes

ADJUSTING THE LEVEL

Down: Before students do the activity, ask the class to give two reasons to support each opinion.

> EXAMPLE
> *City:*
> • You go to many interesting cultural events
> • There are many different kinds of jobs
>
> *Country:*
> • It is better for your health because there is less pollution.
> • Life is more peaceful and calm.

Up: Have students write a paragraph about why they prefer to live in the city or the country. Have students post their paragraphs. Put a paper next to each paragraph so that other students in the class can comment on it.

THEME Entertaining

| 3 | GROUP | DISCUSSION | ▲ |

Language Focus: Talking about customs/culture, using vocabulary for clothing and food

Classroom Tip: Have a class discussion and invite students to share any experiences they have had with the kinds of parties mentioned in the activity.

Time: 10-15 minutes

Answer Key: The following are the most likely answers: *barbecue:* T-shirts and shorts, hamburgers, corn, summer holiday; *potluck supper:* jeans and sweaters, pasta, salads, moving to a new house; *formal dinner:* tuxedo, champagne, wedding; *surprise party:* paper hats, cake and ice cream, birthday; *brunch:* casual or Sunday clothes, eggs, orange juice, weekend morning

ADJUSTING THE LEVEL

Up: Have students each make a chart like that in the book for several kinds of parties in their countries. Have them share their lists with a group and discuss their answers. Ask: *Do students from the same country have similar charts?*

| 4 | PARTNER | INTERVIEW | ⇕ |

Language Focus: Talking about past events, interviewing
Time: 10-15 minutes

ADJUSTING THE LEVEL

Down: Before students do the activity, model it by having students ask you the questions, with volunteers writing the answers on the board.

Up: Have students write up their partner's information in a paragraph. They can ask additional questions if they want to. Their partners then check over the paragraph, making any corrections and adding any information they want.

THEME Humor and Jokes

| 5 | GROUP | DISCUSSION | ⇕ |

Language Focus: Using words with multiple meanings

Classroom Tip: Have dictionaries available so that students can check the meanings of the words in the box.

Time: 10-15 minutes

Answer Key: 1. a clock, 2. coins, 3. a needle, 4. an eye, 5. corn, 6. an envelope, 7. a comb, 8. a chair

ADJUSTING THE LEVEL

Down: Have students use dictionaries to find the multiple meanings of the underlined words.

Up: Have students give both (or at least two) meanings of the words.

> EXAMPLE
> hands — part of the human body at the end of the arm
> hands — the arrows on a clock that point to the time

6 PARTNER INTERVIEW ▼

Language Focus: Talking about personal experiences, giving opinions, interviewing
Time: 15-20 minutes

ADJUSTING THE LEVEL
Down: Before students do the activity, model it by having students ask you the questions, with volunteers writing the answers on the board.

Then brainstorm lists of movies and comedians that students think are funny.

7 GROUP PRESENTATION ⬍

Language Focus: Telling stories, telling jokes
Time: 20 minutes

ADJUSTING THE LEVEL
Down: Have groups practice telling stories and jokes to you and/or to another group before they present them to the class. Provide suggestions for improvement or clarification.

Up: After students do the activity, have them, in small groups, retell the jokes and stories that they thought were the funniest.

INFORMATION GAP Keeping a Budget

8 PARTNER INFORMATION GAP ⬍

Language Focus: Using vocabulary related to farms, using vocabulary related to budgets, asking for and giving information
Time: 15 minutes
Answer Key: Uncle Brendan is in the red by $500.

ADJUSTING THE LEVEL
Down: Before they do the activity, have pairs classify each of the following words as related to finances or to farms: *taxes, seed, salary, fertilizer, expenses, equipment, crops, rent, interest.*

They should use their dictionaries to check any words whose meanings they are unsure of. Check answers as a class and discuss the meaning of the words.

Up: Before students do the activity, write a list of the items in Brendan's budget (from the items in the activity) on the board, mixing the items up. Have pairs classify each item as an expense (money spent) or income (money earned).

PROJECT   APPENDIX 12

Life on a Farm

1 GROUP SURVEY ▼

Language Focus: Using vocabulary related to farms, talking about farm life, using interview skills, making comparisons
Time: 10-15 minutes (In addition, students do fieldwork outside of class.)

ADJUSTING THE LEVEL
Down: Before students do their fieldwork, have them interview someone in class — another student, teacher, or someone else they know who has worked on a farm (and who will come into class). Or, have students brainstorm a list of possible answers to items 3 and 4 before they begin.

2 GROUP RESEARCH ▼

Language Focus: Using various sources to get information, using interview skills, talking about farms, making oral presentations
Classroom Tip: Provide students with the names of farmers' organizations to contact for information. You might also have available in the classroom simple articles about farming with diagrams or a picture dictionary that shows farming vocabulary.
Time: 15-30 minutes (In addition, students do research outside of class.)

ADJUSTING THE LEVEL
Down: To help students with the activity, have the class discuss any experiences they have had with any of the topics. Help students with English vocabulary for farming terms. You might also want to show students information in picture dictionaries related to farming.

EPISODE
37

THANKSGIVING

THEME Family Holidays

| 1 | CLASS | BRAINSTORM | ▲ |

Language Focus: Talking about personal experiences, discussing customs/culture
Time: 5-10 minutes

ADJUSTING THE LEVEL

Up: Have students each write a paragraph about what his/her family usually does on a particular holiday. Ask them to consider these topics:
  • what people wear
  • what people eat
  • what games people play
  • who does the work of preparing and cleaning up for the get-together
Have students share their paragraphs in small groups.

| 2 | PARTNER | INTERVIEW | ▲ |

Language Focus: Talking about personal experiences, discussing customs/culture, interviewing
Time: 10 minutes

ADJUSTING THE LEVEL

Up: Have students work in groups and compare answers. Have them try to answer these questions:
  • Are there any differences in activities according to the countries people are from? If so, what are they?
  • Are there more similarities or differences in the lists?

| 3 | GROUP | DISCUSSION | ▼ |

Language Focus: Reading descriptions to solve a puzzle
Time: 10-15 minutes
Answer Key: Answers will vary, but check for the following: Cousin Jane is not near Dad (she doesn't like smoke); Grandpa Joe is not near Cousin Peter (he doesn't like little children); Mom isn't near Aunt Betty (she doesn't like her); Aunt Betty is across from Cousin Jane.

ADJUSTING THE LEVEL

Down: Illustrate a strategy for helping to solve the puzzle by connecting related pairs of items.
  EXAMPLE
  Dad smokes.
  Cousin Jane doesn't like smoke.
  Conclusion: We shouldn't put Dad near Jane.

THEME Family Secrets

| 4 | PARTNER | ROLE-PLAY | ↕ |

Language Focus: Telling stories
Time: 20-30 minutes

ADJUSTING THE LEVEL

Down: First, have students review the family secret that Rebecca found out from Uncle Brendan.

Then, with the class, brainstorm some possible reasons or scenarios for one or more of the family secrets in the activity:
  EXAMPLE
  First situation
  •The man was your mother's first boyfriend. They were going to get married. But then your mother met your father, and she knew he was the right man for her right away. She broke off the engagement.
  •The man in the picture is your uncle, your mother's brother. You just have never seen a picture of him when he looked so young.
With the class, write a brief role-play based on one of the situations.

Up: After students do the activity, have them each think of a family secret and write a story in a paragraph or in narrative form. It can be based on a secret from real life, the activity, or a book or film, or it can be made up by the student.

THEME Thanksgiving Day

| 5 | PARTNER | MAKING GUESSES | ▼ |

Language Focus: Talking about historical events, making guesses
Time: 10 minutes
Answer Key: 1. 1621, 2. 1789, 3. 1863, 4. 1939

ADJUSTING THE LEVEL

Down: Draw a time line on the board or prepare an overhead. The year 1492 should be at one end of the time line and the current year at the other end. Ask students what the significance of 1492 is (the first Europeans came to the Americas). Mark 1789 on the line and explain that the first president of the United States took office in that year. Invite students to tell any other important dates they know in the history of the United States and mark them on the time line.

| 6 | PARTNER | STORYTELLING | ↕ |

Language Focus: Talking about past events, retelling a story
Time: 15-20 minutes

ADJUSTING THE LEVEL

Down: Guide students through the reading. Ask them to answer these questions after they read each paragraph:
Paragraph 1: Who were Pilgrims? Why did they come to North America?

Paragraph 2: How did the Pilgrims get to North America?
Paragraph 3: What problem did the Pilgrims have when they arrived in North America?
Paragraph 4: What did the Pilgrims have to learn? Who helped them?
Paragraph 5: Why did the Pilgrims celebrate the first Thanksgiving? How did they celebrate it?
Paragraph 6: How did Thanksgiving become a holiday in the United States?

For Part D, help students find the dates in the story. Show them how to calculate the differences and come up with a score, using one pair's answers as an example.

Up: Encourage students to retell the story without looking back at the text in the book. Or, have students make a time line about the story of the Thanksgiving holiday.

GAME **Thanksgiving Football**

7	TEAM	GAME	↕

Language Focus: Asking and answering questions, writing information questions, retelling events from a story
Classroom Tip: Explain a typical football field by copying the game board onto the board or an overhead. Explain that, in football, one team tries to get to one of the goal lines to score a touchdown and the other team tries to get to the other goal line. Using sample questions, demonstrate how teams move up and down the field toward the goal lines.
Time: 15-20 minutes

ADJUSTING THE LEVEL
Down: Review how to form *Who, What, When,* and *Where* questions, mentioning the use of *do/does/did* and the inversion of *be.* To help students form questions, write a list of five or six possible answers on the board, and have the class orally brainstorm questions for the answers.

> EXAMPLE
> A: Guitar lessons.
> Q: What does Rebecca give to Alex and Vincent?
>
> A: Oysters.
> Q: What did the Caseys eat at the restaurant?

Up: Have students play the game again. However, this time students should write definitions of words in English from the video for other students to guess.

> EXAMPLE
> •This is a kind of shellfish. People eat them raw. (oysters)
> •This a popular sport in the United States. People watch this sport on Thanksgiving Day. (football)

Computer Classes

1	GROUP	RESEARCH	↕

Language Focus: Talking about school courses, talking about computers, using interview skills
Time: 5-10 minutes (In addition, students do fieldwork outside of class.)

ADJUSTING THE LEVEL
Down: Before students do the activity, have volunteers talk about common types of computer courses available in schools and describe what the courses teach. Make a list of the courses on the board.

Up: Encourage students to get more information about the courses, such as prerequisites/requirements for entrance, availability of computers at school, number of students in a class, textbooks, and so on.

2	GROUP	SURVEY	↓

Language Focus: Using interview skills, making generalizations
Classroom Tip: Have groups compare answers and, with the class, come up with a profile of a typical student for your school and what the school should teach.
Time: 10-15 minutes (In addition, students do fieldwork outside of class.)

ADJUSTING THE LEVEL
Down: Review the list of courses from Activity 1. Make sure that students understand what the courses teach by having volunteers explain their contents.

EPISODE
38
STARTING OVER

THEME Christmas Bonuses

| 1 | GROUP | SURVEY | ▲ |

Language Focus: Discussing gifts, stating preferences, interview skills
Time: 5-10 minutes

ADJUSTING THE LEVEL
Up: As students do the survey, have them also ask why the person wants a particular Christmas bonus, using the question *Why do you want that bonus?*

| 2 | GROUP | COMPARISON | ▲ |

Language Focus: Discussing gifts, describing personal experiences
Time: 10 minutes

ADJUSTING THE LEVEL
Up: Have groups report overall results to the class in either a pie graph or a bar graph.

| 3 | GROUP | DISCUSSION | ⬍ |

Language Focus: Giving opinions, negotiating
Time: 15-20 minutes

ADJUSTING THE LEVEL
Down: Before students do the activity in their groups, discuss the items as a class. Make a chart listing the positive and negative aspects of each choice.

EXAMPLE
Full-time employees who did great work

Positive	Negative
Rewards those who deserve it	• We have to figure out who did good work. • The people not getting bonuses will be upset.

Up: Have students work in groups of five or six and do a role-play of a meeting of the board of directors. Different students should take different positions.

EXAMPLE
• One person doesn't want any bonuses given.
• One person thinks everyone should have bonuses.
• One person is the chairperson who will decide on what Christmas bonus will be given.

THEME Giving Advice

| 4 | PARTNER | WAYS TO SAY IT | ⬍ |

Language Focus: Giving advice
Time: 10-15 minutes

ADJUSTING THE LEVEL
Down: Before students do the activity, brainstorm a list of possible solutions for each problem.

EXAMPLE
Problem: I feel very stressed and anxious.

Solutions: do less work, get help in your work, set priorities (do the important things first), relax, do something you like to do, listen to music, play a sport, exercise

Up: Have students do a role-play in groups of three — the first student states a problem and the other two students give advice. However, the two students giving the advice don't agree on the best thing to do. Have groups share their role-plays.

| 5 | GROUP | DISCUSSION | ⬇ |

Language Focus: Giving advice
Time: 15 minutes

ADJUSTING THE LEVEL
Down: As a class, brainstorm two pieces of advice for each problem. In the groups, students can choose between the two pieces of advice to give Harry or think of some advice of their own.

THEME Losing a Job

| 6 | GROUP | DEBATE | ⬍ |

Language Focus: Giving opinions, talking about work issues
Time: 15 minutes

ADJUSTING THE LEVEL
Down: To prepare students to do the activity, have students think of things that Rebecca and Emma could say about the situation and the job.

EXAMPLE
Rebecca: I really need a job. When I left, it was an emergency. I didn't know when I would be back. I am good at the job. The children like me.

Emma: I had to hire someone else. There was no one to work with Rebecca's group of children at that time. It was unfair to the parents. They pay for our program, and they want their children to play and learn. It was unfair to the other workers in the program, too: they had to do Rebecca's job, as well as their own.

Up: Have students do a follow-up debate relating to work issues that they suggest; for example, the types of benefits that all employees should get.

| **7** | **PARTNER** | **DISCUSSION** | ⬍ |

Language Focus: Reading want ads, discussing job requirements, giving opinions
Time: 10-15 minutes

ADJUSTING THE LEVEL
Down: Tell students to analyze the jobs according to these criteria:
- Does Rebecca have the right experience for the job?
- Are the hours good for Rebecca?
- Will the job help her in her future career?

Up: Present actual help-wanted ads to students and see if they can find a good job for Rebecca. You might want to obtain pages from help-wanted ads and put them on overheads.

INFORMATION GAP
Decorating a Christmas Tree

| **8** | **PARTNER** | **INFORMATION GAP** | ⬍ |

Language Focus: Describing locations, asking for and giving information
Time: 10-15 minutes

ADJUSTING THE LEVEL
Down: Before students do the activity, draw a Christmas tree on the board or on an overhead. Draw ornaments similar to those in the activity. Describe the placement of a few of the ornaments on the tree, and then invite volunteers to do the same. Write the following words on the board to help students in their descriptions:
- above
- below
- next to
- to the right of
- to the left of
- between
- at/near the bottom of
- at/near the top of
- in the middle of

Up: Have students do a similar follow-up activity. Each student draws a Christmas tree with ornaments. Then he/she makes a copy of it, leaving out some of the ornaments. Students then give the copy to their partner, and the pair work together to fill in the missing ornaments.

Sports for Children

| **1** | **PARTNER** | **SURVEY** | ⬍ |

Language Focus: Discussing sports, using interview skills
Time: 10-20 minutes (In addition, students do fieldwork outside of class.)

ADJUSTING THE LEVEL
Down: To prepare students for the activity, have students discuss the sports that children play in their country and the benefits of each for children.

Up: In addition to interviews with children and parents, have students interview people who work with children and sports, such as gym teachers in schools or people who run after-school programs. When students report results, have them debate whether the opinions of these people should count more in making decisions about the sports program than the opinions of children or parents.

EPISODE
39

THE PRESSURE'S ON

THEME Managing Priorities

| 1 | GROUP | DISCUSSION | ⬍ |

Language Focus: Discussing everyday activities, giving reasons
Time: 15-20 minutes

ADJUSTING THE LEVEL

Down: To simplify the activity, have groups first do the following:
- List the three most important things for Rebecca to do
- List the three least important things for Rebecca to do

Then have them use these decisions to help them choose the six items for their lists.

Up: Have each group write up a schedule for Rebecca's Tuesday night and present it the class, explaining reasons for choices. The group should include any phone calls she should make. Have the class vote on the best schedule.

THEME Stress

| 2 | PARTNER | INTERVIEW | ▲ |

Language Focus: Talking about personal experiences
Time: 5-10 minutes

ADJUSTING THE LEVEL

Up: Have students continue the interview. Students are to think of a particularly stressful time in their lives. Partners ask each other the following questions:
- What was the most stressful time in your life?
- What caused all the stress?
- What finally happened to change your situation?

Alternatively, during the interview, have partners ask follow-up questions such as these:
- Why does school cause you stress?
- Why does your family cause you stress?

| 3 | PARTNER | STRESS TEST | ⬍ |

Language Focus: Discussing everyday events, discussing personal experiences
Time: 10 minutes

ADJUSTING THE LEVEL

Down: Before students do the activity, have them make up sentences with *often, sometimes,* and *never,* using information from Activity 2. Write sentence frames such as the following on the board to guide students:

I _____ feel stress because of school.
I _____ feel stress because of my car.

Up: Before students do the activity, have them predict how they think they will score. After they do the activity, have them discuss results — and any surprises — with their partners.

| 4 | GROUP | SURVEY | ⬍ |

Language Focus: Discussing everyday activities, sharing personal experiences
Time: 10-15 minutes

ADJUSTING THE LEVEL

Down: Before students do the activity, have the class brainstorm a list of common ways in which people relieve stress. Write the list on the board.

Up: As a follow-up activity, write the following letter on the board or on an overhead. Have each student write a letter in response, giving advice about how to deal with stress.

EXAMPLE
Dear Miss Advice,
I often feel stressed. I work eight hours a day. I go to school three nights a week to learn English. I am worried about doing a good job at work. I am worried about doing a good job at school. I am always working and worrying.

Post students' letters. Have the class vote on some of the best responses.

THEME Being Direct

| 5 | PARTNER | WAYS TO SAY IT | ⬍ |

Language Focus: Giving direct answers to problem situations, discussing problem situations
Time: 10-15 minutes

ADJUSTING THE LEVEL

Down: Go over the expressions in the box. Then present situations like those in Activity 5 and have students give frank answers, using the expressions in the box.

EXAMPLE
T: Do you mind if I smoke in here?
Ss: To be perfectly honest, I wish you wouldn't.

Other questions:
- Is it all right if I leave class early?
- Can I turn on the rock and roll radio station?
- Can I borrow your dictionary?
- Does my dog bother you?

Up: Have students develop role-plays of at least six exchanges for one or two of the situations in Activity 5, or for one of their own.

6 | PARTNER | DISCUSSION ▼

Language Focus: Discussing everyday situations, giving opinions, discussing customs/culture
Time: 10 minutes

ADJUSTING THE LEVEL

Down: Before students do the activity, discuss the situations as a class. After students do the activity, have them discuss the reasons for their answers.

Present some situations when it is OK to be direct in American culture and have students discuss any differences with what is done in their countries:

- People can refuse to grant permission for someone to smoke.
- People can refuse to answer personal questions, such as *How old are you?* or *How much money do you make?*
- Friends can often say whether or not they like something that a friend is thinking of buying.
- Teachers can tell students when they are not performing well. They usually do this in a private meeting with the student.

GAME **Studying for Exams**

7 | GROUP | GAME ↕

Language Focus: Talking about school, talking about everyday activities
Time: 20-30 minutes (Students can play the game several times during the episode.)

ADJUSTING THE LEVEL

Down: Have students brainstorm study tips as a class. Students can use the list of tips as they prepare the game cards.

Up: After students play the game, have each group come up with a list of the five best study tips and a list of five things not to do when studying. Groups should present and explain their lists, answering any questions from the class. Have the class vote on the best set of tips.

Opera

1 | PARTNER | RESEARCH ▼

Language Focus: Using sources to get information, summarizing a story
Classroom Tip: Provide information on one or more musical works. The explanations found on CDs would be a possible source, as would music encyclopedias.
Time: 10 minutes (In addition, students do research outside of class.)

ADJUSTING THE LEVEL

Down: Do the activity with the class. Select a musical work. You can play parts of it and display material from various sources, such as a CD jacket or an encyclopedia. With the class, model the activity. Help students find the information needed to complete the chart in the activity.

2 | CLASS | STORYTELLING ↕

Language Focus: Telling stories, making oral presentations
Time: 20-30 minutes

ADJUSTING THE LEVEL

Down: Have pairs of students give their presentations to one another before they give it the class. The pairs should ask questions of one another, asking about anything that was not clear or indicating any other information that they would like to have.

Up: Encourage students to give more detail about the characters in the opera and about the composer.

E P I S O D E
40
SHARING FEELINGS

THEME
Things That Are Important to You

1 | GROUP | RANKING

Language Focus: Giving opinions, expressing preferences
Classroom Tip: After the activity is finished, have groups report results, telling their top three answers. Find the most common answers given by the class.
Time: 10-15 minutes

ADJUSTING THE LEVEL
Down: After students do the activity, help them summarize results by writing the following sentence frames on the board and having students complete them:

To most students in my group, _____ is important.
To many students in my group, _____ is important.
To some students in my group, _____ is important.
To only a few students in my group, _____ is important.

Up: Before students do the activity, have individual students write what they think the group's answers will be. Have students report the survey results for their group in a suitable form, such as in a line or bar graph or in a simple paragraph. Have groups discuss similarities/differences.

2 | PARTNER | INTERVIEW

Language Focus: Giving opinions, interviewing
Time: 5-10 minutes

ADJUSTING THE LEVEL
Down: Before students do the activity, have the class brainstorm other things that they think are important in people's lives.

EXAMPLE
• being in good health
• having a special talent

Up: Have students write a paragraph in which they tell about three things that are important in their lives right now. Have students share paragraphs with their partners.

THEME **Being Patient or Impatient**

3 | CLASS | BRAINSTORM

Language Focus: Discussing everyday experiences
Time: 5-10 minutes

ADJUSTING THE LEVEL
Down: Before doing the activity as a class, have students work in pairs and try to answer the following questions: *Think back over the last week. In what situations have you waited? How long did you wait?* Have students share their lists of situations as they brainstorm as a class.

4 | GROUP | SURVEY

Language Focus: Talking about everyday experiences, giving personal opinions, interviewing
Time: 5-10 minutes

ADJUSTING THE LEVEL
Up: Have students work in pairs and interview a partner about a time he or she had a long wait and what happened. For example, it might have been waiting to hear the results of exams, waiting for a vacation to come, waiting for someone to meet him/her, or waiting to get an official document like a visa. Guide students with these questions:
• What was the situation when you were impatient?
• When did it happen?
• How long did you have to wait?
• How did you feel while waiting?
• When did the wait finally end?
Students report their partner's experiences to another pair.

5 | GROUP | DISCUSSION

Language Focus: Discussing everyday experiences
Time: 10 minutes

ADJUSTING THE LEVEL
Down: Introduce the activity by telling of personal experiences when it was good to be patient (when waiting for someone or something important, such as an important visitor or a job interview), and impatient (when someone who was sick needed help and wasn't getting it, or when someone promised to do something important right away and didn't do it).

Discuss how people in the United States show how they are impatient by physical gestures (tapping feet or sighing), or by complaining in a loud voice. Discuss any cultural differences that students may have noticed as to how and when people in different cultures show impatience.

THEME **Making Money**

6 | PARTNER | BRAINSTORM

Language Focus: Discussing everyday experiences, giving information
Classroom Tip: Pair students of higher and lower language proficiency.
Time: 15 minutes

ADJUSTING THE LEVEL

Down: With the class, discuss ways people make money other than employment.

1. Explain the pictures at the right (a business, investments in the stock market, an invention) and how people can make money from them.
2. Encourage students to think of how people they know have been successful in earning money. Share any examples that you know about.

Make a class list of ways to make money and write it on the board before students do the activity. Remember to remind students to give specific examples and details as they work with their partners.

| 7 | TEAM | GAME | ⬍ |

Language Focus: Negotiating, giving reasons
Classroom Tip: Before students play the game, make sure that no two teams have chosen the same or very similar ideas.
Time: 15 minutes

ADJUSTING THE LEVEL

Down: Before students put their five ideas on the board, have them present them to the class.

Up: Before students play the game, have individual students come up with a list of the five items they would choose. Have students present their lists and tell why they want the items, trying to persuade the other members of their team. The team makes its choices after listening to all the presentations.

INFORMATION GAP
Rock and Roll Music

| 8 | PARTNER | INFORMATION GAP | ⬇ |

Language Focus: Reading reviews, using the vocabulary of music, asking for and giving information
Classroom Tip: Begin with a discussion about rock and roll and about some of the more famous bands and musicians from this musical style. You might want to have some CD covers or pictures of rock and roll groups available to show the class.
Time: 15 minutes

ADJUSTING THE LEVEL

Down: To prepare students for the activity, have them brainstorm words related to music in the following categories:
- Musical instruments
- Musical styles
- Names of CDs they know in English

Also review words for expressing opinions:
- Adjectives: *great, fantastic, wonderful*
- Verbs: *I like this. / I recommend this.*

Invite volunteers to tell about one or two of their favorite albums, incorporating the language.

P R O J E C T   APPENDIX 4

Using the Library

| 1 | GROUP | RESEARCH | ⬍ |

Language Focus: Getting information, summarizing information
Time: 5-10 minutes (In addition, students do fieldwork outside of class.)

ADJUSTING THE LEVEL

Down: Do the activity as a class field trip. You might want to have a librarian present some of the information, but have students do items 7 and 8 on their own.

Up: Have students add other interesting information that they find out about the library.

| 2 | PARTNER | RESEARCH | ⬍ |

Language Focus: Using various sources to get information
Time: 5-10 minutes (In addition, students do research outside of class.)

ADJUSTING THE LEVEL

Down: Before students do the activity, as a class, brainstorm likely places/sources where students can find the answer to each item.

Up: Have each pair make up five similar questions to give to another pair. Of course, the pair has to have an actual source for each answer (written on a separate piece of paper)!

As an alternate, make up a list of ten questions that would interest the students. (Make sure sources with the answers are available to students.) Have a "treasure hunt." The first pair to find all the answers and give the sources is the winner!

E P I S O D E
41

UNEXPECTED OFFERS

T H E M E **Moving to a Different Country**

| 1 | GROUP | BRAINSTORM | |

Language Focus: Discussing personal experiences, making generalizations
Time: 10 minutes

ADJUSTING THE LEVEL
Down: Before students do the activity, have them discuss any personal experiences they have had moving to a new country by asking the following questions:
- When you moved to a new country, what changes did you have to make?
- What things were different to you or new to you in the country you moved to?

After experiences are presented, ask students to find any similarities.

Up: Have students work in pairs and interview each other about any experiences they have had moving to or visiting another country.
- What things in the new country surprised you?
- What things were hard for you to do?
- What problems did you have when you first arrived?
- What things did you have to learn?
- What did you miss about your country?
- What did you like about the other country?

Students report their partner's answers/story to another pair.

| 2 | PARTNER | INTERVIEW | ▲ |

Language Focus: Making comparisons, interviewing
Time: 5-10 minutes

ADJUSTING THE LEVEL
Up: Have students get together with their groups from Activity 1 and predict the class's top three answers to Activity 2. As a class, tally the answers (to Activity 2) and ask groups to compare their predictions with the actual results.

T H E M E **Invitations**

| 3 | PARTNER | WAYS TO SAY IT | |

Language Focus: Inviting, accepting or refusing invitations
Time: 10-15 minutes

ADJUSTING THE LEVEL
Down: Review the language in the boxes. Prepare two sets of cards. One set has invitations; the other set has cards with either the words *yes/accept* or the words *no/refuse*. Have students work in pairs. Partners should not choose from the same set. The pairs act out a role-play according to the information on the cards.

> EXAMPLE
> Invitation cards: go to lunch together, work on a project together, come to a party at my house, go out for dinner
> A: (card = go to lunch together) Would you like to go to lunch?
> B: (card = yes/accept) Yes. I'd like that.

Have pairs repeat the activity several times.

Up: Have students prepare role-plays of invitations for people in the video. Here are some ideas:
- Rebecca asks Bill to study in the library.
- Bill asks Rebecca to go for a coffee after the audition.
- Alberto asks Rebecca to go to the opera with him.
- Nancy asks Rebecca to go to the retirement home with her to visit Edward.
- Rebecca asks Angela to go to lunch at a café with her.

| 4 | PARTNER | MATCHING | ▲ |

Language Focus: Reading invitations, understanding customs/culture
Time: 5-10 minutes
Answer Key: 1. d (✔), 2. b, 3. c (✔), 4. a (✔), 5. e, 6. f

ADJUSTING THE LEVEL
Up: Have students work in small groups and discuss situations in which they send written invitations in their countries. Tell them to discuss the information they put on invitations. Encourage them to compare and contrast their customs with U.S. customs for sending written invitations. Finally, have students come up with a summary of what they learned from one another and share the results with the class.

T H E M E **The Christmas Spirit**

| 5 | CLASS | DISCUSSION | ▼ |

Language Focus: Discussing customs/culture
Time: 10-15 minutes

ADJUSTING THE LEVEL
Down: Discuss some of the customs associated with Christmas in the United States:
- giving gifts to friends (clothing, games, jewelry, and so on)
- giving food and clothing to those who need it
- giving to charities (for example, donations of toys or clothing)

As a lead-in to the class activity, ask students if they know of any other holidays or periods with any of these customs or with similar customs.

Language Focus: Persuading others, giving reasons
Time: 20-30 minutes

ADJUSTING THE LEVEL
Down: Have students discuss the work of each of the groups on the list. Choose one (preferably one not being used by any of the student groups) and model the activity: discuss the nature of the charity, the good things it does, and reasons people should contribute to it. Write the information on the board. Then model how to give a presentation incorporating this information.

GAME **Giving Christmas Presents**

7 | TEAM | GAME | ⇕

Language Focus: Discussing gifts, using vocabulary for gifts
Time: 15 minutes
Answer Key: Each person's present begins with the same letter as the person's first/last name and it has the same number of letters as the person's first name: Saul Sills, skis; Susanna Sills, sweater; Sally Sills, snake; Samuel Sills, skates; Carson Chills, camera; Cindy Chills, clock; Caroline Chills, computer; Cal Chills, cat; Brian Bills, books; Brenda Bills, blouse; Ben Bills, bat; Beatrice Bills, baseball; Tom Tills, tie; Thalia Tills, ticket; Teddy Tills, train; Tallulah Tills, tricycle.

ADJUSTING THE LEVEL
Down: Before students do the activity, have them look at the objects on the page for one minute. Then have students work in pairs and list as many of the objects as they can remember.

Up: After students play the game, have them write a paragraph about the gift they would most like to receive and why. Post the paragraphs in the classroom and invite other students to guess who wrote each paragraph.

PROJECT APPENDIX 5

Vacations

1 | PARTNER | RESEARCH | ▼

Language Focus: Using various sources to get information
Classroom Tip: Have available travel-related information, such as brochures or guidebooks. For variety, make sure that each group chooses a different place to report on.
Time: 10 minutes (In addition, students do research outside of class.)

ADJUSTING THE LEVEL
Down: Model doing the activity for a place to which you would like to go. If possible, have available travel brochures or guidebooks with information to answer the questions, and help students to find the answers.

2 | PARTNER | PRESENTATION | ⇕

Language Focus: Describing places, making oral presentations, expressing personal preferences
Time: 20-30 minutes

ADJUSTING THE LEVEL
Down: Have pairs give their presentations to other pairs. Have pairs ask about anything they don't understand and say whether they feel they have enough information to decide if they want to visit the place.

Up: As students listen to the presentations, have them write one interesting fact from each presentation. After the presentations, have students work in small groups and share their lists.

E P I S O D E
42
THE AUDITION

THEME Waiting

| 1 | CLASS | BRAINSTORM | |

Language Focus: Discussing everyday situations
Time: 10 minutes

ADJUSTING THE LEVEL
Down: Have students discuss the situations in the pictures for the activity. Have them answer these questions:
- What is each person waiting for?
- What would you do in similar situations?

Up: Before students do the activity as a class, have students work in pairs and make their own lists of everyday situations in which people wait.

| 2 | GROUP | SURVEY | |

Language Focus: Giving opinions
Time: 10-15 minutes

ADJUSTING THE LEVEL
Up: As a follow-up, have students rank the list by how often (very often, sometimes, never) they personally wait in each of the situations. Have them try to find out if there is a connection between how often they wait and what they hate waiting for.

| 3 | PARTNER | INTERVIEW | |

Language Focus: Getting information
Time: 5-10 minutes

ADJUSTING THE LEVEL
Down: Have students do a follow-up activity. Have them make a list of three situations in which they waited a long time and give the times. Have students share their lists in small groups.

Up: Have students work in small groups and discuss differences and similarities in cultures they know about relating to time. Have them answer these questions:
- Do people wait a lot? In what situations do people commonly wait and expect to wait?
- Are people usually on time for business appointments? for school? for social events?
- Are there situations where people seldom wait in one country and where people commonly do in another?
Have groups share conclusions and examples from their discussion as a class.

| 4 | CLASS | DATA ANALYSIS | |

Language Focus: Making comparisons, giving personal reactions
Time: 10-15 minutes

ADJUSTING THE LEVEL
Down: Supply language for the class to discuss results by writing the following sentence frames on the board:
> The class average to wait for _____ is _____ minutes.
> I would wait longer than that.
> I wouldn't wait longer than _____ minutes for that.

Have students work in small groups and rank the importance of waiting for the items in Activity 3 and any others they would like to add. Have groups present their answers to the class.

Up: Before the activity, have pairs predict the average waiting time. After the activity, find the pair that was closest to the class average. (Pairs should find the difference between their guess and the class average for each item and then add all the numbers.) The pair with the lowest number wins.

THEME The Importance of Education

| 5 | CLASS | DISCUSSION | |

Language Focus: Giving personal opinions
Time: 10-15 minutes

ADJUSTING THE LEVEL
Up: Choose one of the five items. Have students raise their hands according to the answer they gave for that item. Students with the same answer form groups. Each group comes up with reasons and examples from real life to support its opinion and shares the information with the class. Do this with two or three items.

| 6 | GROUP | ROLE-PLAY | |

Language Focus: Giving opinions, persuading
Time: 15 minutes

ADJUSTING THE LEVEL
Down: Before students do the activity, have them list reasons that the child and parents can give and write them on the board. Then model how to do the role-play with volunteers, first playing the child and then a parent.

| 7 | GROUP | PRESENTATION | |

Language Focus: Giving opinions, persuading
Time: 20-30 minutes

ADJUSTING THE LEVEL
Down: Before students do the activity, have them answer this question as a class: *Why do you want to learn English?*

THEME An Audition

| 8 | CLASS | GAME | ▼ |

Language Focus: Engaging in everyday conversations
Time: 20-30 minutes

ADJUSTING THE LEVEL

Down: Before students do the activity, brainstorm a list of good situations from the video to use in their auditions.

Then, with a volunteer, model the conversation between Rebecca and Alberto at the gallery. Take these positions:
- At first, Rebecca is nervous being at a gallery. Give Rebecca's response to seeing the picture of Alex and Ramón. Give Rebecca's response to seeing her picture.
- Alberto wants Rebecca to see his photographs, but he wants her to be surprised.

Have students consider these questions as they prepare their role-plays:
- What does my character want to say?
- What is my character feeling?
- What is going to happen at the end?

SONG Dream Catcher

| 9 | PARTNER | SONG | ▼ |

Language Focus: Interpreting a song, understanding figurative meanings
Time: 15 minutes
Answer Key: 1. b, 2. c, 3. b, 4. c, 5. The singer wants the dream catcher to catch her., 6. The person who is a "dream catcher" can help another person when things are going badly.

ADJUSTING THE LEVEL

Down: Review the meaning of a dream catcher. It is a Native American object made of string and feathers. The Native American legend says that a dream catcher stops bad dreams but lets good dreams go through.

Go over the words of the song with students. Discuss these questions as a class:
- What problem does the singer have?
- What does she want? Why?

| 10 | GROUP | DRAWING | ▲▼ |

Language Focus: Describing a scene, describing art
Classroom Tip: Have art supplies such as paper, paint, crayons, markers, and colored pencils available, or ask students to bring them in.
Time: 15-20 minutes

ADJUSTING THE LEVEL

Down: To simplify the activity, discuss the question in Part A as a class. Then have students work in pairs. You might want to pair students who have more artistic ability with those who are less artistic. Circulate as students are drawing and ask them what they are drawing and why.

Up: Have students do the same activity for another song that they know in English. In their presentations, have students both play the song and explain their pictures.

| 11 | TEAM | GAME | ▲▼ |

Language Focus: Talking about music
Time: 10 minutes

ADJUSTING THE LEVEL

Down: Before students do the activity, play one or two sad songs or blues songs in English. Explain what the lyrics are saying and discuss any new vocabulary. Ask the students their opinions of the song.

Up: After students do the activity, have them tell about the contents and lyrics of some of the songs. Then ask teams to choose a song from the list for a presentation. In the presentation, they should summarize the lyrics of the song and, if possible, play it for the class.

PROJECT   APPENDIX 6

Dedication

| 1 | PARTNER | RESEARCH | ▼ |

Language Focus: Using various sources to get information, reporting information, giving oral presentations
Classroom Tip: If possible, have simple English-language biographies or encyclopedias available.
Time: 20-30 minutes (In addition, students do research outside of class.)

ADJUSTING THE LEVEL

Down: Choose a person for whom you have material available, or have the class choose a person they admire and obtain materials about him or her. With the class, go through the sources to obtain the information. Then, with the class, paraphrase the information needed to answer the questions and write the answers on the board.

E P I S O D E
43

DREAM CATCHER

THEME **Success**

| 1 | PARTNER | RANKING | ▲ |

Language Focus: Giving personal opinions, interviewing
Classroom Tip: After students do the activity, have them report their answers to obtain overall results — i.e., the items that are ranked "Very important" on most lists.
Time: 10 minutes

ADJUSTING THE LEVEL

Up: Ask students to come up with a list of two or three things that typically mean "success" in their home countries/cultures.

Have students work in groups and share their lists. They should discuss these questions:
- What things do most people in my country think are important for success? What things do people in the United States think are important for success?
- What are the differences between the two countries in the ways people think about success? What are the similarities?

THEME **Talent**

| 2 | CLASS | BINGO | ↕ |

Language Focus: Discussing abilities, giving personal information, interviewing
Classroom Tip: After students do the activity, go over each item in the squares, have students raise their hands if they can do it, and make a tally of how many students can do each item.
Time: 15 minutes

ADJUSTING THE LEVEL

Down: Before students do the activity, have them work in pairs and tell what talents on the board they each have. For this lead-in activity, try to pair students of higher and lower language proficiency. Have students count the number of things they each can do. Find the student with the highest total. Go over any unfamiliar vocabulary before starting the activity.

Up: Have the students work in groups and make a list of 19 items to put on their own bingo cards. Have each student write up a card, using the same 19 items. Have students exchange cards with another group to use in a follow-up game.

| 3 | GROUP | ROLE-PLAY | ▼ |

Language Focus: Discussing personal abilities, persuading others
Time: 20 minutes

ADJUSTING THE LEVEL

Down: Before students do the activity, as a class, brainstorm abilities that might be useful on the spaceship and why. Write lists like the following on the board.

> EXAMPLE
> *tell jokes:*
> People on the spaceship will need to laugh. They are in a very stressful situation.
> *perform first aid:*
> People on the ship and the new planet will need medical attention.
> *know how to program a computer:*
> We will need to write new computer programs to solve new problems.

THEME **Having Confidence**

| 4 | GROUP | BRAINSTORM | ↕ |

Language Focus: Giving reasons, giving personal opinions, talking about occupations
Time: 10 minutes

ADJUSTING THE LEVEL

Down: Before students do the activity, have them brainstorm reasons why the following people need confidence:
- teachers
- TV reporters
- athletes

Up: As students do the activity, have them list two reasons why each group needs confidence.

| 5 | GROUP | INTERVIEW | ▼ |

Language Focus: Giving opinions, interviewing
Classroom Tip: After students do the activity, take a tally to see how many students think each item is true or false.
Time: 10-15 minutes

ADJUSTING THE LEVEL

Down: Before students do the activity, have them ask you for your opinions. Explain your answers by giving examples.

After students do the activity, choose one of the five items. Have students raise their hands according to the answer they gave for that item. Students with the same answer should form groups. Each group comes up with reasons and examples from real life to support its opinion and shares the information with the class. Do this with two or three items.

6 | TEAM | GAME

Language Focus: Using English vocabulary words, spelling
Time: 10 minutes

ADJUSTING THE LEVEL

Down: Encourage students to use a dictionary to check the spellings of words.

Up: Have students both write the words and explain why the words are included. They should use a separate piece of paper for their sentences.

> EXAMPLE
> • college — Rebecca is going to the San Francisco <u>College</u> of Music.
> • opera tickets — Alberto gets <u>opera tickets</u> as a Christmas bonus.
> • Nancy — <u>Nancy</u> is Rebecca's godmother.

INFORMATION GAP   Taking a Message

7 | PARTNER | INFORMATION GAP

Language Focus: Using telephone language, asking for and giving information, taking notes
Time: 10-15 minutes

ADJUSTING THE LEVEL

Down: Model doing the activity. Copy the message pad on the board or on an overhead. Ask students to copy it on a piece of paper. You give the following message. Students are to ask questions to get the information they need to fill out the form. Each student should fill out his/her own form. Then go over the answers together.

> EXAMPLE
> You had plans to meet your friend, Anita, at a restaurant after work today. You need to stay longer at work today. You will still meet her — but one half-hour later. You will meet her at the restaurant at 6:30, not at 6:00.

Up: Have pairs take all of the messages, using a separate piece of paper.

Then have the pairs make up their own message. Tell them to think of messages they have taken or given recently. Each pair then prepares a role-play in which one gives the message to the other. The pair presents it to a group. The members of the group listen carefully and take down the message they hear on separate pieces of paper.

Chocolates

1 | PARTNER | RESEARCH

Language Focus: Using sources to get information
Time: 5-10 minutes (In addition, students do research outside of class.)

ADJUSTING THE LEVEL

Down: You may want to present students with sources that supply the information and put them on overheads or read them to the students. The students take notes to answer the questions.

Up: Have the class brainstorm two or three questions to add to the list of questions and try to answer them in their research.

> EXAMPLE
> • What kinds of chocolate are popular in _____?
> • How is chocolate made?
> • What countries produce the most cocoa beans?

2 | GROUP | SURVEY

Language Focus: Discussing culture/customs, using interview skills, reporting information
Time: 15-20 minutes (In addition, students do fieldwork outside of class.)

ADJUSTING THE LEVEL

Down: Have volunteers tell about special uses of candy in their countries. Use the information given to illustrate how to fill out the chart in the activity.

EPISODE
44

GIFTS

THEME **The Community Center**

1 | GROUP | DISCUSSION | ▲

Language Focus: Discussing community needs, negotiating
Time: 10-15 minutes

ADJUSTING THE LEVEL

Up: Have each group write two or three sentences about why it made the choices it did. Have the groups answer these questions:

- Why is this item important to help the community?
- Why is it important for a community center to provide this service?

2 | CLASS | POLL | ▲

Language Focus: Discussing community needs, presenting choices
Time: 10 minutes

ADJUSTING THE LEVEL

Up: Have students also tell why they made the choices they did, using their answers from the Adjusting the Level — *Up* suggestions in Activity 1. Then have students discuss the following items:

- In their countries, which of the services on the list are often provided by government?
- Which are provided by religious groups?
- Which are provided by private charity groups?

Point out that in the United States, private groups often provide these services.

3 | PARTNER | PUZZLE | ⬍

Language Focus: Using food vocabulary, reading information to solve a puzzle
Time: 15 minutes
Answer Key: 1st floor, Meal B; 2nd floor, Meal D; 3rd floor, Meal C; 4th floor, Meal A; 5th floor, Meal E

ADJUSTING THE LEVEL

Down: Before students do the activity, have them group the following food items into the correct categories in the chart: chicken, beef, hamburger, cheese, ice cream, soda, cake.

Meat: _____
Dairy Products: _____
Sweets: _____

Show one way of solving the puzzle:
EXAMPLE
The person who can't eat beef lives on the first floor, so that person shouldn't get meals D and E. The vegetarian lives on the 4th floor. He lives below the person who can't eat milk products. The person who can't eat milk products is on the top floor. That person shouldn't get Meal A or Meal D.

Up: Have students explain their answers.
EXAMPLE
From the first and fourth clues, we know that the vegetarian lives on the 4th floor. So Meal A goes to him. All the other meals have meat. The person who can't eat sweets lives below the vegetarian, so he lives on the 3rd floor. He gets Meal C because he wants chicken. Meal B has chicken but it has sweets, . . . and so on.

THEME **Breaking Up**

4 | GROUP | OPINION SURVEY | ▲

Language Focus: Giving opinions, interviewing
Time: 10-15 minutes

ADJUSTING THE LEVEL

Up: Extend the interview by having students ask the following questions:

- Why do you think people can be friends after they break up?
- Why do you think it is easy/hard for people to be friends after they break up?

Have students give reasons for their answers.
EXAMPLE
Reasons you can be friends: You really like the other person. You may have a lot of interests in common. You know a lot about the person.
Reasons it is hard to be friends: It may make you jealous to see the person with someone else.

5 | PARTNER | DATA ANALYSIS | ⬍

Language Focus: Making generalizations, making comparisons
Classroom Tip: After the activity is finished, have groups report results and add up the votes to find overall results for the class.
Time: 10 minutes

ADJUSTING THE LEVEL

Down: After pairs complete the activity, have them say which of the following statements are true and which are false, according to the information they have from their groups.

1. More than half the women think that people can be friends after they break up.
2. More than half the men think that people can be friends after they break up.
3. Less than half the women think that people can be friends after they break up.
4. Less than half the men think that people can be friends after they break up.

5. Less than half of the men and women think that people can be friends after they break up.
6. More than half of the men and women think that people can friends after they break up.

Up: After pairs do the activity, have them work in their groups from Activity 4 to report group results in graph form, such as in bar or circle graphs. Have groups compare graphs.

THEME Inspirations

6	PARTNER	WRITING	▼

Language Focus: Writing a paragraph, discussing personal experiences, interviewing
Time: 20-30 minutes

ADJUSTING THE LEVEL
Down: With the class, brainstorm personal inspirations. Encourage volunteers to share inspirations like those suggested in the directions for the activity, or by other situations; for example, they saw someone doing something well — taking pictures, or swimming — and they wanted to do the same thing themselves.

Then model the activity. Have students ask you the questions and have volunteers write your answers on the board. Then, as a class, write a paragraph that incorporates your answer.

GAME Skiing

7	TEAM	GAME	▲

Language Focus: Reviewing vocabulary, spelling words
Classroom Tip: Before teams play the game, model the guessing activity by choosing a few words, writing blanks on the board, and asking students to guess letters to figure out the words (for example, *college, audition, restaurant, architect*).
Time: 20-30 minutes (The game can be played several times during the episode.)

ADJUSTING THE LEVEL
Down: Give students this tip for playing the game. They should write down the letters of the English alphabet. As guesses of letters are made, they can cross the letters out.

Up: The students must both guess the words and tell how they relate to the *Connect with English* video. Teams have to give at least two sentences for each word. The teacher is the judge of correct sentences.

> EXAMPLE
> Ramón gives Alberto a nice pair of goggles. Alberto can use the goggles on his ski trip.

PROJECT   APPENDIX 8

Helping People in the Community

1	GROUP	RESEARCH	↕

Language Focus: Using various sources to get information, using interview skills
Time: 20-30 minutes (In addition, students do research and fieldwork outside of class.)

ADJUSTING THE LEVEL
Down: You may want to model the activity by talking about a service organization or by providing information about it on an overhead. Students can answer the questions in Part B in writing.

To further simplify the activity, you might want to provide students with names, addresses, and phone numbers of local organizations which they can research.

Up: Have two groups work together. Each group writes an article for a school newspaper about the organization that the other group researched in Part A. Have each group post its article.

E P I S O D E
45
TRUE LOVE

THEME   An Ekeko

1   PARTNER   INTERVIEW

Language Focus: Talking about personal experiences and wishes, interviewing
Time: 10-15 minutes

ADJUSTING THE LEVEL
Down: Before students do the activity, discuss as a class the possible meaning of each of the items pictured in Activity 1.
> EXAMPLE
> •diploma — a degree in computers
> •ring — marriage
> •passport — travel
> •pen — writing something that is published
> •star — becoming famous
> •heart — finding someone to love

As a class, brainstorm a list of wishes and possible ekeko items to go with each wish.

Up: Have individual students write a paragraph in which they explain their choices of ekeko items. Have pairs share their paragraphs.

2   TEAM   GAME

Language Focus: Describing things
Time: 20-30 minutes

ADJUSTING THE LEVEL
Down: Model how to do the activity with the items presented.
> EXAMPLES
> guitar
> Player A: It's a musical instrument. It has strings. Rebecca has one.
> Player B: It's a guitar.
>
> tennis racket
> Player A: It's used to play a sport. It has strings.
> Player B: It's a soccer net.
> Player A: No, you use it to hit a ball.

3   CLASS   DISCUSSION

Language Focus: Describing items, describing personal experiences and wishes
Time: 20-30 minutes

ADJUSTING THE LEVEL
Down: Have students give their explanations of the ekekos in groups of three before they give them to the class. The others in the group ask questions about things that they don't understand and they give any help with needed vocabulary.

Up: Have students work in pairs and write an article for a school newspaper article describing the ekeko activity that the class did. They should report on the most common and most unusual items.

THEME
Exchanging Christmas Presents

4   PARTNER   WAYS TO SAY IT

Language Focus: Expressing appreciation and thanks
Time: 10 minutes

ADJUSTING THE LEVEL
Down: Go over the expressions in the box. Then have each student write the name of a gift that he or she would like on a piece of paper, as well as his or her name. Students take turns drawing a paper at random and presenting the "gift" (the paper) to the student whose name is on the paper. The second student thanks the first for the "gift."

Up: Have the students work in pairs and do role-plays of various characters in the video as they receive gifts. The pairs perform their role-plays, with the class trying to guess the characters and the gift. Here are some suggestions of situations to role-play:
• Rebecca — receiving car or necklace from her Dad
• Rebecca — receiving the photograph from Alberto
• Uncle Brendan — receiving the ring from Rebecca
• Ramón — receiving the tape from Rebecca

5   GROUP   DISCUSSION

Language Focus: Talking about likes and interests, describing people
Time: 20-30 minutes

ADJUSTING THE LEVEL
Up: Have the students think of a funny present and a serious present for each person, as they do the activity. An example of a funny present would be a chocolate soccer ball, for someone who likes chocolate and soccer.

THEME   Falling in Love

6   PARTNER   DISCUSSION

Language Focus: Discussing reasons, discussing personal characteristics
Classroom Tip: Have partners report their choices to the class. List the two most common reasons that students have given for why each of the characters — Ramón and Rebecca — is falling in love.
Time: 5-10 minutes

ADJUSTING THE LEVEL

Up: Have pairs present their choices and their reasons for their choices to the class. Have the class find the four most popular choices for both Ramón and Rebecca. With the class, make a list of information from the video to support each reason. Then have the class vote for the two best reasons for each character.

| 7 | GROUP | DISCUSSION | ▲ |

Language Focus: Giving personal opinions, discussing reasons for actions
Time: 10-15 minutes

ADJUSTING THE LEVEL

Up: Have the groups write reasons for their opinions, in addition to their choices.

> EXAMPLE
> *Kindness:* We think kindness is a good reason to fall in love. A kind person will be a good spouse. You will be able to count on the person to help you and understand your problems.
>
> *Fame:* We don't think that fame is a good reason to fall in love. In fact, it might be difficult to have a famous person as a husband or wife. You can't have a normal home life because fans will want to know everything you do.

INFORMATION GAP **Planning a Trip**

| 8 | PARTNER | INFORMATION GAP | ▼ |

Language Focus: Asking for and giving information, reading about travel, reading descriptions of places
Time: 15 minutes

ADJUSTING THE LEVEL

Down: Have Student As and Student Bs work in separate groups. Student As work on page 5 and Student Bs work on page 6. Groups work on completing the following chart for each of the three tours on their page:

Places the tour goes	
Things you do with the tour group	
How long the tour is	
Cost of the tour What is included in the cost	

Students can refer to the charts as they do the information gap activity.

PROJECT

Legends

| 1 | GROUP | RESEARCH | ▼ |

Language Focus: Reading legends, summarizing a story in writing
Classroom Tip: Have available books about legends. Illustrated books and books for children might provide material written at a language level appropriate for students.
Time: 10 minutes (In addition, students do research outside of class. You may want to allow class time for groups to write their summaries of legends.)

ADJUSTING THE LEVEL

Down: Model how to do the activity by reading a legend aloud or presenting it on an overhead and having students summarize it as a class.

Here are some questions that students can answer in their summaries:
- Who are the characters?
- What are the magical events?
- What happens at the end?
- What does the legend explain?

| 2 | GROUP | POSTER | ⬍ |

Language Focus: Retelling stories, making oral presentations, describing events
Classroom Tip: Have materials for making posters available, including large sheets of paper and colored pencils, markers, or crayons.
Time: 20-30 minutes (You may want to allow class time for groups to prepare their posters and descriptions.)

ADJUSTING THE LEVEL

Down: Have groups present a description of what they plan to draw to another group before they put it on their poster. The other group asks questions about things they don't understand or things they would like more information about.

Up: Have students discuss legends from their countries that are similar to the legends they heard about in class.

E P I S O D E

46

FRIENDSHIP

THEME Being Impressed

1 | PARTNER | RANKING | ▲

Language Focus: Giving opinions, talking about things that impress people, interviewing
Time: 10-15 minutes

ADJUSTING THE LEVEL

Up: Have students write a separate paragraph for each of the two things on the list of things that impress them the most and tell why. Have students share their paragraphs in small groups.

2 | CLASS | BRAINSTORM | ↕

Language Focus: Talking about personal knowledge and experiences
Time: 5-10 minutes

ADJUSTING THE LEVEL

Down: Have students think about the kinds of things they do to impress people and the kinds of things that impress them. Discuss these questions as a class:
- Has anyone impressed you in the last week? What happened?
- Think of people you know who impress you. Why do they impress you?

Up: Have students do the activity in pairs and then share their lists with the class.

3 | PARTNER | COMPARISON | ▲

Language Focus: Talking about personal knowledge and experiences, giving opinions
Time: 10 minutes

ADJUSTING THE LEVEL

Up: Have each pair prepare a role-play in which one partner tries to impress the other by doing the items on their lists. Have pairs present their role-plays in small groups.

THEME Collecting Autographs

4 | GROUP | DISCUSSION | ↕

Language Focus: Making generalizations, describing groups of people
Time: 10 minutes

ADJUSTING THE LEVEL

Down: Do the activity as a class. Some other possible groups are actors, writers, political leaders, and TV personalities. Help students with spellings of proper names.

Up: Have students each write a paragraph about the person whose autograph they would most like to have and tell why. Post students' paragraphs and invite other students to read the paragraphs and write their reactions next to them.

5 | CLASS | GAME | ↕

Language Focus: Talking about personal experiences
Classroom Tip: After the game, have the ten students whose items are on the board tell their stories. Provide help as necessary.
Time: 10 minutes

ADJUSTING THE LEVEL

Down: Have students work in pairs. They should help each other decide on the most interesting experience each has had. They then help their partners write about their experiences.

After you have written the items for the activity on the board, explain them. Model how to ask an appropriate question for several items on the board.

> EXAMPLE
> see a famous actor
> Did you ever see a famous actor?

Up: After the class plays the game, have the ten students whose items are on the board tell their stories, as suggested above. Have students who are listening write a summary of the experience that they think is the most interesting and share their summary with a partner.

THEME Sharing Good News

6 | PARTNER | WAYS TO SAY IT | ↕

Language Focus: Telling good news, reacting to good news
Time: 10-15 minutes

ADJUSTING THE LEVEL

Down: Before students do the activity, write the expressions on the board. Also, write a list of good-news items like the following:
1. I just got a new job.
2. I just found a nice apartment.
3. I got an A in my English class.
4. I just sold my old car at a good price.
5. I just got engaged to my girlfriend/boyfriend.

Tell the good news and have individual students respond to it. Then have individual students give the news, while other students respond to it.

Up: Have students think of some real piece of good news that they have had lately and tell it in groups. The other students in the group should respond appropriately to the news.

Language Focus: Giving good news, reacting to good news
Time: 15 minutes

ADJUSTING THE LEVEL

Down: Before students do the activity, brainstorm a list of 10 to 15 pieces of good news as a class. These items can then be used in the activity.

Up: As students do the activity, they should vary both the news and the responses. Before this, brainstorm a list of positive reactions as a class, such as *That's wonderful! / That's fantastic. / You're so lucky. / I am happy for you. / Get out of here!*

GAME **The Music Business**

| 8 | TEAM | GAME | ⬍ |

Language Focus: Asking questions, talking about music, writing questions
Time: 30-40 minutes

ADJUSTING THE LEVEL

Down: Model writing several questions with the class. Then invite students to suggest the names of songs and singers to incorporate in the questions.

Up: Students can vary the questions. They can ask about singers, lyrics, and so on.

> EXAMPLE
> Who were the members of the Beatles?
> a. Paul McCartney, John Lennon, Ringo Starr, George Harrison
> b. Paul McCartney, John Lennon, Yoko Ono, Ringo Starr
> c. John Lennon, Mick Jagger, Paul McCartney, Ringo Starr

PROJECT APPENDIX 10

Languages

| 1 | GROUP | RESEARCH | ⬆ |

Language Focus: Using various sources to get information, using language names
Time: 5-10 minutes (In addition, students do research outside of class.)

ADJUSTING THE LEVEL

Up: Have students in each group write three additional facts that they find out about languages and share them with another group.

| 2 | TEAM | GAME | ⬇ |

Language Focus: Using language names, using interview skills
Time: 20 minutes

ADJUSTING THE LEVEL

Down: Allow students to interview other students in class and people outside of class. Write the following questions on the board to guide them as they do the activity:
- What languages do you speak?
- What languages do you know at least a few words from?
- Can you show me how to write "hello" in that language?
- Can you tell me how to say it?

E P I S O D E
47
THE LOST BOYS

THEME Changing Plans

| 1 | PARTNER | INTERVIEW | ▲▼ |

Language Focus: Talking about everyday situations, interviewing
Time: 10-15 minutes

ADJUSTING THE LEVEL
Down: Discuss the situations as a class before students give their answers. Have volunteers tell their answers and why.

Up: Before students do the activity, have them discuss times when they changed their plans during the last month. Have them tell why. With the class, make a list of reasons why people change plans:
  • The weather is bad.
  • Something else more important comes up (a relative is sick).
  • At the last moment you don't feel like going out.
Have students discuss times when it is good to change plans and times when it isn't.

THEME Baby-sitting

| 2 | GROUP | WRITING INSTRUCTIONS | ▼ |

Language Focus: Writing instructions
Time: 10-15 minutes
Answer Key: Answers will vary. Here are some likely answers: John shouldn't eat chocolates. Give John an apple to eat. Put John to bed at 9:00. Give John his medicine before you put him to bed. You can eat the ice cream in the refrigerator. John can watch videos, or he can draw, or he can read books.

ADJUSTING THE LEVEL
Down: Before students do the activity, present the language for giving instructions:

EXAMPLE
You / The child should _____.
You / The child shouldn't _____.
You can _____.
Don't _____.
Please _____.

With the class, brainstorm a list of common instructions for baby-sitting.
EXAMPLE
• Please put John to bed at 9:00.
• John shouldn't watch TV.
• You can eat the food in the refrigerator.
• You should give John his medicine.

THEME Children and Money

| 3 | PARTNER | PUZZLE | ▲▼ |

Language Focus: Talking about types of money
Time: 10-20 minutes
Answer Key:
1. 3 quarters + 2 pennies
2. 3 quarters + 3 nickels + 5 pennies,
   or 2 quarters + 4 dimes + 5 pennies,
   or 2 quarters + 9 nickels,
   or 8 dimes + 3 nickels,
   or 1 quarter + 4 dimes + 6 nickels
3. 1 quarter + 2 dimes + 1 nickel + 3 pennies
4. 1 half-dollar + 1 dime + 1 nickel + 1 penny
Bonus question:
3. 1 quarter + 2 dimes + 1 nickel + 1 penny
4. 1 quarter + 1 dime + 3 nickels + 1 penny
5. 1 quarter + 5 nickels + 1 penny
6. 5 dimes + 1 penny
7. 4 dimes + 2 nickels + 1 penny
8. 3 dimes + 4 nickels + 1 penny
9. 2 dimes + 6 nickels + 1 penny
10. 1 dime + 8 nickels + 1 penny
11. 10 nickels + 1 penny

ADJUSTING THE LEVEL
Down: Go over the coins and their value. Do a sample item with the class and show how to solve it.

EXAMPLE
26 cents, 2 coins

It must be a quarter and a penny.
25 cents + 1 cent = 26 cents
1 quarter + 1 penny = 2 coins

Up: Have pairs write problems like those on the page and have other pairs solve them.

| 4 | PARTNER | INTERVIEW | ▲ |

Language Focus: Talking about customs/culture, talking about personal experiences
Time: 10 minutes

ADJUSTING THE LEVEL
Up: Have pairs come up with a list of three good rules for parents to follow when they give money to their children.

EXAMPLE
- Children should earn the money they get by doing chores.
- Children should get an allowance every week. It should not be more than ____.
- Children should be encouraged to save money.
- Children should be able to spend their allowance on anything they want.

Pairs should share their lists.

| 5 | PARTNER | ROLE-PLAY | ▼ |

Language Focus: Giving reasons, persuading
Time: 15-20 minutes

ADJUSTING THE LEVEL
Down: Brainstorm reasons that either child or parent might give in order to persuade the other.

Child:
- I want to buy a computer. I can use the computer for games, but the computer can help me with my schoolwork, too.
- I know that you need to clean the garage. I'll help you clean it and keep it clean.

Parent:
- I need to save money to buy a car for the family.
- You have bought several expensive things and then not used them very much.

Model doing the activity as a class, taking first the role of the parent and then that of the child.

INFORMATION GAP
Missing Person's Report

| 6 | PARTNER | INFORMATION GAP | ▼ |

Language Focus: Describing a person, asking for and giving information
Time: 15-20 minutes

ADJUSTING THE LEVEL
Down: With the class, brainstorm a list of words to describe people. Write the list on the board.

EXAMPLE
Height: tall, short, medium
Weight: Heavy, thin, average
Hair: long, short, curly
Hair color: blond, black, red, brown
Clothing: jeans, white shirt, athletic shoes, tie, green jacket

Then show a picture of a person (such as one from a magazine) and work with the class to fill out a missing person's report on the person in the picture. Use the chart in the activity as a model.

Ice Skating

| 1 | PARTNER | RESEARCH | ⬍ |

Language Focus: Using sources to get information, talking about sports
Time: 5-10 minutes (In addition, students do research outside of class.)

ADJUSTING THE LEVEL
Down: To simplify the activity, you might find an encyclopedia article or an almanac that has the answers to the questions. Have the pairs try to find the answers.

Up: Have students find the answers to additional questions, either ones that interest them or ones like the following.

EXAMPLE
- What is ice dancing?
- How is figure skating organized at the Olympics?
- How is figure skating scored at the Olympics?

| 2 | PARTNER | RESEARCH | ▼ |

Language Focus: Getting information, talking about sports
Time: 20 minutes (In addition, students do research outside of class.)

ADJUSTING THE LEVEL
Down: For Activity B, show how to calculate the speeds over the various distances by the formula:

distance traveled ÷ time = the speed (rate) of travel

Have students discover who travels the fastest by determining the rate traveled in various sports for each distance.

E P I S O D E
48

A VERY GOOD YEAR

THEME New Year's Resolutions

1 | PARTNER | INTERVIEW | ▲

Language Focus: Talking about personal intentions, interviewing
Time: 10 minutes

ADJUSTING THE LEVEL

Up: Have students write a paragraph on one of the following topics:
- A New Year's Resolution I Kept
- A New Year's Resolution I Didn't Keep
- Why I Don't Make New Year's Resolutions

Have students share their paragraphs in small groups.

2 | CLASS | GAME | ▲

Language Focus: Talking about personal intentions, explaining guesses
Time: 10 minutes

ADJUSTING THE LEVEL

Up: After students do the activity, have them discuss why some answers were easy or hard for them. For example, there may have been several people with the same resolution, which made it hard to guess. Or they may know some students well enough to be certain of their resolutions, which made it easy to guess.

Then have students vote on the "winners" in the following categories of resolutions:
- The one hardest to keep
- The one easiest to keep
- The silliest one
- The one I really would like to make and keep

3 | CLASS | DISCUSSION | ↕

Language Focus: Discussing personal intentions, discussing study tips
Time: 20 minutes

ADJUSTING THE LEVEL

Down: Before students do the activity, have the class brainstorm some good tips for learning English, such as listening to videotapes or audiotapes, writing summaries of films they see in English, and so on.

Up: After students do the activity, have them each write a list of good tips for learning English. Have them work in groups of three and come up with a master list of ten good tips. Then have the groups pool tips and come up with a master list for the class. Post the list somewhere in the classroom for everyone to see.

THEME Trust

4 | PARTNER | TRUST TEST | ↕

Language Focus: Giving personal information, discussing personal qualities, interviewing
Time: 10-15 minutes

ADJUSTING THE LEVEL

Down: Give a dictionary definition of trust: to believe that someone is honest and will not hurt you or cheat you. Discuss with students situations where it might not be a good idea to trust someone; for example, when someone you don't know asks you for a favor.

Up: Extend the activity by having pairs answer this question for each situation: *Is it a good idea to trust the person in Situation 1?* Have pairs form small groups and compare answers and defend the ones they have given.

THEME Parenting

5 | PARTNER | SURVEY | ▲

Language Focus: Giving opinions, discussing personal experiences, interviewing
Time: 10-15 minutes

ADJUSTING THE LEVEL

Up: As students do Part A of the activity, have them write reasons for their examples.

> EXAMPLE
> I don't want to give my child $20 for a video because that is expensive. He/she may watch it once and never watch it again.

Then gather class results into two groups. For each item, find the answers given by those students who have children versus the answers given by students who do not have children. Have students try to analyze and explain any similarities or differences.

6 | CLASS | DEBATE | ▼

Language Focus: Giving reasons
Time: 20-25 minutes

ADJUSTING THE LEVEL

Down: Have students discuss whether they think their parents were too strict with them and give reasons. (An alternate idea would be to have students discuss whether they think that parents in the United States are too strict or too relaxed with their children.)

As a class, discuss the example in the video:
- What did Alex and Vincent do that was wrong?
- How is Ramón going to punish Alex?
- Do you think that Ramón is too strict with Alex?
- Ramón lets Alex go the New Year's party. Do you think that Ramón is too lenient with Alex?

GAME **Grounding**

Language Focus: Discussing people's behavior, making judgments about people's behavior, using vocabulary for common activities
Time: 20-30 minutes

ADJUSTING THE LEVEL
Down: Before students start the activity, check that they understand key vocabulary by asking them to complete the following matching activity:

1. cheat   a. leave home
2. lie   b. take something that is not yours
3. run away   c. not tell the truth
4. spill   d. when liquid pours out of a container by accident
5. steal   e. do something dishonest to win or gain something

Up: Have students play the game again with a list of at least ten bad behaviors that they brainstorm as a class.

  EXAMPLE
  • not obeying you when you tell the child to clean his/her room or do an important chore
  • saying something mean to a relative
  • not attending a family party
  • not doing his/her homework
  • taking money you give him/her to buy groceries and spending it on something for himself/herself

PROJECT   APPENDIX 12

New Year's Eve

| 1 | PARTNER | RESEARCH | ▼ |

Language Focus: Talking about customs/culture, getting information from sources, using interview skills
Classroom Tip: You might have information about New Year's celebrations available in the classroom, particularly materials that are at the appropriate language level.
Time: 10 minutes (In addition, students do research outside of class.)

ADJUSTING THE LEVEL
Down: Before students do the activity, have them give the information for one or two cultures they know. Write a master list of answers on the board.

| 2 | CLASS | PRESENTATION | ⬍ |

Language Focus: Talking about customs/culture, making oral presentations
Time: 20-30 minutes

ADJUSTING THE LEVEL
Down: Before each pair gives its presentation to the class, it should present it to another pair, who will ask questions about anything that is unclear.

Up: Have students discuss similarities and differences among the New Year's celebrations.

ORAL EVALUATION CHECKLISTS

This section contains checklists which can be used to assess students' mastery of the language proficiency objectives promoted by the activities in the *Conversation Books*. There are 12 checklists in all — one for every four episodes in the *Conversation Books*.

How to Use the Checklists

The checklists should be administered after students have viewed the corresponding four video episodes and have completed the activities in the *Conversation Books*. The themes and language objectives that are being tested are conveniently listed on each checklist.

1. **Make a copy of the checklist for each student.** This way you can keep individual evaluations and notes on each student's performance.

2. **Administer the checklists during one-on-one sessions.** These can take place outside the classroom or in the classroom as other students engage in other activities such as group work. Administration time generally should not exceed 5-10 minutes per student. In addition, you may want to skip the proficiencies/themes that were not covered in class.

3. **For each objective, read the script in italic type aloud to the student.** In some cases, you will be asked to engage students in role-plays. In such cases, suggestions for role-play openers and language are given.

4. **Circle the score that you think best represents the student's mastery of each objective.** These scores range from 0 to 3, and represent the students' ability to respond and perform each language objective.

Using the Scores

The scores can be used to get a general picture of student progress. If a student's scores are mostly 0 and 1, this indicates that he or she may not have gained mastery of this particular objective. If a student's scores are consistently 2 and 3, this, on the other hand, indicates that he or she is making good progress.

You can use the scores on the checklists, together with your observations of a student's performance/proficiency in class and written homework, to give the student a grade for the class. These scores can also aid in grouping students according to language proficiency.

STUDENT NAME _____

KEY: 0 = does not meet the objective   1 = meets the objective with difficulty
       2 = meets the objective adequately   3 = meets the objective with ease

OBJECTIVES

SCORE/NOTES

1. Talking about Personal Dreams and Plans
Theme: Pursuing Your Dreams — Episode 1

Answer these questions:
- *What is Rebecca's dream for the future?*
- *What is your dream for the future?*
- *What are you doing to make your dream come true?*

0 1 2 3

2. Talking about Friendship/Giving Personal Opinions
Theme: Friendship — Episode 2

Part 1: *Answer these questions:*
- *What are two things a good friend does?*
- *What are two things a good friend never does?*

0 1 2 3

Part 2: *Think about a good friend of yours. Why is he or she a good friend?*

0 1 2 3

3. Talking about Customs and Personal Habits — Food
Themes: Making a Shopping List — Episode 2; Barbecue — Episode 3

Answer these questions:
- *What are some foods that you buy every week?*
- *What are some foods that people eat at barbecues?*
- *What are some foods that people eat at parties in your country?*

0 1 2 3

4. Talking about Jobs
Themes: Career Choices — Episode 3; What's Your Job? — Episode 3
Role-Play
*We are going to do a role-play. We are at a party. We meet each other for the first time.
I will ask you questions about your job and you will tell me about it. You can choose
any job you like.*
Note: *Ask questions such as What do you do for a living? Where do you work?
What do you do at your job? What is your favorite part of the job?*

0 1 2 3

5. Expressing Congratulations
Themes: Expressing Congratulations — Episode 4; Getting Accepted — Episode 4

Part 1: *Please respond to my statements. Congratulate me.*
- *I have good news. I just got engaged.*
- *I have good news. My son just graduated from school.*

0 1 2 3

Part 2: *Name one thing that happened to you for which you received congratulations.*

0 1 2 3

6. Talking about Family Relationships
Theme: Different Types of Families — Episode 4

Part 1: *Answer these questions:*
- *Who is the oldest person in your family? Who is the youngest?*
- *How many cousins do you have?*
- *How many people are unmarried in your family?*

0 1 2 3

Part 2: *Describe some of the people in your family. Tell me how you are related
to them.*

0 1 2 3

STUDENT NAME _____

KEY: 0 = does not meet the objective   1 = meets the objective with difficulty
       2 = meets the objective adequately   3 = meets the objective with ease

OBJECTIVES

SCORE/NOTES

1. Describing Preferences — Clothing
Themes: A Shopping Mall — Episode 5; Formal and Informal Clothes — Episode 5

0 1 2 3

Part 1: *Answer these questions:*
• *What would you wear to an elegant restaurant?*
• *What would you wear to a barbecue?*

0 1 2 3

Part 2: *Answer these questions:*
• *Where do you usually go to buy clothes?*
• *Do/Would you like to shop in shopping malls? Why or why not?*

0 1 2 3

Part 3: Role-Play
We are going to do a role-play. You are going to a wedding in an elegant hotel. You want to buy clothes for the occasion. You are in a store. I am a salesperson. Tell me what you need and I will ask questions and make suggestions.
Note: Ask questions from Episode 5, page 4, such as *What would you like to wear?*

2. Saying Goodbye
Theme: Saying Goodbye to Friends — Episode 6

0 1 2 3

Role-Play
We are going to do a role-play. You and I have worked together in an office for four years. I am leaving the company because I have gotten a job in another city. It's my last day and I am leaving the office.

3. Talking about Customs and Personal Habits — Food
Theme: Junk Food — Episode 6

0 1 2 3

Answer these questions:
• *What did you eat yesterday?*
• *What healthy foods did you eat?*
• *Did you eat any junk foods? (if yes) What were they?*

4. Talking about Surprises
Theme: Surprises — Episode 7

0 1 2 3

Please respond to my statements. Express surprise.
• *I have good news. I just won $5,000 in the lottery.*
• *You have won a brand new car!*

5. Expressing Personal Preferences — Presents
Theme: Presents — Episode 7

0 1 2 3

Part 1: *Answer these questions:*
• *What are two presents that you would like to receive?*
• *What are two presents that you would like to give?*

0 1 2 3

Part 2: Role-Play
We are going to do a role-play. You are in a department store. You are shopping for a present for your best friend's birthday. I am a salesperson. Tell me what you are thinking of buying for your friend.

6. Talking about Personal Experiences — Fears
Theme: Being Afraid — Episode 8

0 1 2 3

Answer this question:
Is there anything that you are afraid of? What is it?

STUDENT NAME _____

KEY: 0 = does not meet the objective   1 = meets the objective with difficulty
       2 = meets the objective adequately   3 = meets the objective with ease

OBJECTIVES

SCORE/NOTES

1. Making Polite Requests
Themes: Being Polite — Episode 9; Taking Photos — Episode 11,
Cultural Differences — Episode 12

Part 1: Make a request for each of these situations:
• *You want your teacher to repeat the homework assignment.*
• *You want to take a picture of some friends at a party.*
• *You want to use a friend's telephone to make a call.*

0 1 2 3

Part 2: Role-Play
We are going to do a role-play. We are both living at a boarding house. You want to watch a movie on television. I am in the living room of the boarding house, where the television is. I am listening to music.

0 1 2 3

2. Using the Telephone
Theme: Answering Machines — Episode 9

Role-Play
We are going to do a role-play. You are calling me on the telephone. You need to tell me that you will come to my house to study tonight, but you will be late. You will come at seven o'clock and not six o'clock. If I am not home, leave a message on my answering machine.
Note: Answer the phone in this way. Hello. This is _____. I can't come to the phone right now. Please leave a message. Thank you.

0 1 2 3

3. Bargaining
Themes: Bargaining — Episode 10; Selling Your Car — Episode 10

Part 1: Role-Play
We are going to do a role-play. Look at the picture of the car. (Show Episode 10, page 4.) You want to sell the car to me for $10,000. Here are ideas to consider:
• *Tell me how much mileage the engine has.*
• *Tell me about some of the options on the car, such as air conditioning and air bags.*
Note: In this role-play, try not to spend more than $8,000 for the car.

0 1 2 3

Part 2: Role-Play
Now we are going to do another role-play. This time you want to buy the car. You don't want to spend more than $7,000.

0 1 2 3

4. Buying a Ticket
Theme: Taking a Bus Trip — Episode 11

Role-Play
We are going to do a role-play. Look at the bus schedule. (Show Episode 11, page 3.) You want to buy a round-trip bus ticket to Chicago. You want to leave in the morning. I am the clerk at the bus station. Ask for the ticket.

0 1 2 3

5. Talking about Personal Habits/Preferences — Boarding Houses
Theme: Living in a Boarding House — Episode 12

Answer this question:
Would you like to live in a boarding house? Why or why not?

0 1 2 3

ORAL EVALUATION CHECKLIST

EPISODES 13–16

STUDENT NAME_____

KEY: 0 = does not meet the objective   1 = meets the objective with difficulty
     2 = meets the objective adequately   3 = meets the objective with ease

SCORE/NOTES

OBJECTIVES

1. Giving Directions
Theme: Giving Directions — Episode 13

0 1 2 3

Part 1: Role-Play
*We are going to do a role-play. (Show Episode 13, page 1.) We are here.
(Point to "You Are Here.") I am going to ask for directions. You tell me how
to get to the places.*
- *How do I get to the library?*
- *How do I get to Northwood Inn?*

Part 2: Ask the student to give you directions from your school to some place nearby.

0 1 2 3

2. Expressing Sympathy
Theme: Having a Bad Day — Episode 14

0 1 2 3

Part 1: *Respond to my statements. Express sympathy.*
- *I've had a bad day. My car broke down and I was late for my first class.*
- *I've had a bad day. I lost my wallet.*

Part 2: *Answer this question:*
When you have a bad day, what makes you feel better?

0 1 2 3

3. Making a Date/Giving an Invitation
Theme: Making a Date — Episode 14

Role-Plays
We are going to do two role-plays.
*1. You are having a party on Saturday night at 8:00 at your home. Call me on
the phone and invite me to the party.*
Note: For this role-play, accept the invitation.

0 1 2 3

*2. I will invite you to go to the movies tomorrow night at 9:00.
There's a good comedy film at the movie theater near school. You can't go.*

0 1 2 3

4. Giving a Compliment
Theme: Giving Compliments — Episode 15

0 1 2 3

Give me a compliment. You really like my _____.
(Choose a piece of clothing you are wearing.)

5. Making Suggestions
Theme: Making Suggestions — Episode 15

0 1 2 3

I am having some problems. Give me some suggestions.
- *I have a cold.*
- *I don't have anything to do this weekend.*

6. Talking about Personal Experiences
Theme: The First Day of Class — Episode 16

0 1 2 3

Tell me about the first day of this class. What did you do the first day?

7. Talking about Personal Characteristics
Theme: Making New Friends — Episode 16

0 1 2 3

*We are meeting for the first time. Tell me a few things about yourself. Include
these topics: your interests, your work, your favorite music or sport.*

CHECKLIST **4**

ORAL EVALUATION CHECKLIST

STUDENT NAME _____

KEY: 0 = does not meet the objective   1 = meets the objective with difficulty
       2 = meets the objective adequately   3 = meets the objective with ease

OBJECTIVES

SCORE/NOTES

1. Giving Personal Information/Spelling
Themes: Filling Out Forms — Episode 17; Spelling — Episode 17

Role-Play
(If possible, use an actual form, such as a registration form for your school.)   0 1 2 3
We are going to do a role-play. You are registering at a school for English classes.
I work at the school, and I need some information. Answer these questions:
- *What's your last name?*
- *Can you spell that?*
- *What's your first name?*
- *Can you spell that?*
- *Where do you live?*
- *How many years have you studied English?*

2. Talking about Likes/Dislikes — Art
Theme: Appreciating Art — Episode 18

(Show students Book 3, Episode 27, page 3. If Book 3 is not available, use two of the
paintings in Book 2, Episode 18, page 2, or two pictures of paintings from other books.)   0 1 2 3
Point to each painting and ask:
What do you think of this painting?

3. Talking about Everyday Activities — Leisure Activities
Theme: Having Fun — Episode 19

Answer this question:
What do you like to do for fun in your free time?   0 1 2 3
Note: Ask follow-up questions, such as *What kinds of movies do you like to see?* or
How often do you go dancing?

4. Getting Information about People
Theme: Getting Close to Someone — Episode 19

Role-Play
We are going to do a role-play. I am Rebecca/Ramón.   0 1 2 3
We have recently met. You want to get to know more about me.
Ask me questions. Here are some ideas. Ask what I usually do on Saturdays. Ask about
the sports I play. Ask about the kinds of music and films I like. Continue the conversation
by asking at least four questions.
Note: Respond by using the information in Episode 19, pages 5 and 6, or make up information.

5. Apologizing
Theme: Apologizing — Episode 20

Make apologies for these situations.
- *You forgot to call your friend yesterday. You see your friend at school.*   0 1 2 3
- *You said that you would meet your friend at three o'clock at a restaurant.*
You arrive at 3:30.

STUDENT NAME_____

KEY: 0 = does not meet the objective   1 = meets the objective with difficulty
        2 = meets the objective adequately   3 = meets the objective with ease

OBJECTIVES

SCORE/NOTES

1. Talking about a Daily Schedule
Theme: A Daily Schedule — Episode 21

0 1 2 3

Part 1: *Answer these questions:*
- *What is your daily schedule like?*
- *What do you usually do from 6:00 a.m. to 9:00 a.m.?*
- *What do you usually do from 9:00 a.m. to 12 noon?*
- *What do you usually do from 6:00 p.m. to 9:00 p.m.?*

0 1 2 3

Part 2: *Now answer these questions:*
- *Do you think your schedule is too busy?*
- *Do you have enough free time?*
- *How would you like to change your schedule?*

2. Persuading
Theme: Being Stubborn — Episode 21

0 1 2 3

Role-Play
We are going to do a role-play. I am a friend of yours. I want you to go out with me tonight and see a movie. You really don't feel like going out. I'll try to make you change your mind.
Note: Begin the exchange with:
Hi, ____. I'd like to go the movies tonight. Why don't you come with me?
Here are some reasons to give as the conversation continues:
People say it's a funny movie. You'll laugh for sure. You need to get out. It will make you feel better. You shouldn't stay in all the time. It will be fun. It will take your mind off other things.

3. Solving Problems/Giving Advice
Theme: Solving Problems — Episode 21

0 1 2 3

I have some problems. Tell me what to do.
- *My car is getting old. I don't know if I should buy a new one or fix it.*
- *I need to save money. I don't know how to do it.*

4. Accepting a Gift
Theme: Accepting a Gift — Episode 22

0 1 2 3

What would you say? You have given someone in class several rides home. One day, he/she gives you a gift in a wrapped package.

5. Talking about Personal Experiences — Moving
Theme: Moving Away — Episode 23

0 1 2 3

Have you ever moved? (if yes) Where did you move from? Where did you move to? What did you miss about your old home? (if no) If you could move anywhere in the world, where would you move? Why?

6. Talking about Personal Preferences — Parties
Theme: Parties — Episode 24

0 1 2 3

Answer these questions:
- *What do you like to do at parties?*
- *What do people usually do at parties in your country?*

STUDENT NAME_____

KEY: 0 = does not meet the objective   1 = meets the objective with difficulty
        2 = meets the objective adequately   3 = meets the objective with ease

OBJECTIVES

SCORE/NOTES

1. Talking about Personal Experiences
Theme: Remembering Good and Bad Times — Episode 25

Tell me about a good time in your life.
Tell me about a bad time in your life.
       0 1 2 3

2. Talking about Everyday Activities — Cleaning the House
Theme: Cleaning the House — Episode 26

Answer these questions:
- *Which housecleaning jobs do you usually do?*
- *Which housecleaning jobs do you like the least?*
       0 1 2 3

3. Talking about First Aid
Themes: First Aid — Episode 26; Medical Emergencies — Episode 26

Role-Play
We are going to do a role-play. I am going to ask you about a medical problem.
Tell me what to do. Use the information in the book. (Show Episode 26, page 4.)
I just burnt my hand. I tried to pick up a hot pot. What should I do?
       0 1 2 3

4. Negotiating
Theme: Living Together — Episode 27

Role-Play
We are going to do a role-play. We are going to share an apartment. Let's decide how
we will do or share the following things:
- *buying groceries*
- *cooking*
- *watching TV*
Note: Prompt students with questions such as *What should we do about buying groceries?*
       0 1 2 3

5. Apologizing and Forgiving
Theme: Forgiving — Episode 28

Part 1: *Please respond to my statements.*
I am sorry. I forgot to return the book you lent me.
       0 1 2 3
Part 2: *I am a friend. I am so sad. You forgot that yesterday was my birthday.*
Apologize to me.
       0 1 2 3

6. Asking for and Giving Personal Information
Theme: Reunions — Episode 28

Role-Play
We are going to do a role-play. I am an old friend of yours. I haven't seen you in many
years. Answer my questions.
- *Where do you live now?*
- *What kind of job do you have?*
- *How is your family?*
       0 1 2 3

STUDENT NAME_____

KEY: 0 = does not meet the objective   1 = meets the objective with difficulty
       2 = meets the objective adequately   3 = meets the objective with ease

SCORE/NOTES

OBJECTIVES

1. Talking about Personal Experiences
Theme: Memories — Episode 29   0 1 2 3

Part 1: *Answer these questions:*
Can you remember your first English class? What was it like? What did you study?   0 1 2 3
Part 2: *Can you remember any of the following from when you were a child?*
Tell me about one of the things:
- a favorite animal   • a scary experience
- a fun place to visit   • a special gift

2. Describing Emotions
Theme: Expressing Emotions — Episode 29   0 1 2 3
Complete the sentences:
- It makes me feel nervous when _____.
- It makes me feel scared when _____.
- When I am sad, I usually _____.
- When I am angry, I _____.

3. Talking about Plans
Theme: Making Plans for the Future — Episode 30   0 1 2 3
Part 1: *Answer these questions:*
- What are you going to do after you finish this class?
- What are you going to do on your next vacation?   0 1 2 3
Part 2: *Think about your plans for the future. Tell me about them.*

4. Talking about Spending Money
Theme: Spending Money — Episode 31   0 1 2 3
You got $50,000 from a relative who has died. How will you spend the money?

5. Talking about Likes and Dislikes
Theme: Likes and Dislikes — Episode 32   0 1 2 3
Answer the questions:
- What is something you really like? Tell me why.
- What is something you don't like to do? Tell me why.

6. Giving Information — Restaurants
Theme: Restaurants — Episode 32   0 1 2 3
Part 1: Role-Play
*We are going to do a role-play. (Show students Episode 32, page 6.) I am looking
for an Italian restaurant that costs less than $15 per person. Can you tell me the
name of one? Can you tell me the address?*
Part 2: Role-Play   0 1 2 3
Note: Don't refer to the book for this role-play.
*I am looking for a good place to eat in this neighborhood. Can you recommend
a good restaurant? (Ask follow-up questions about food, price, and address.)*

STUDENT NAME _____

KEY: 0 = does not meet the objective   1 = meets the objective with difficulty
        2 = meets the objective adequately   3 = meets the objective with ease

OBJECTIVES

SCORE/NOTES

1. Talking about Personal Experiences
Theme: Favorite Places — Episode 33

Think about a favorite place of yours. Do you have a favorite place to go and think?
Do you have a favorite place to go for fun? Tell me about one of your favorite places.
What does it look like? What do you do there?

0 1 2 3

2. Talking about Personal Preferences
Theme: Keeping in Touch — Episode 33

Answer this question:
How do you keep in touch with family and friends who are far away?

0 1 2 3

3. Making Compromises
Theme: Making Compromises — Episode 34

Role-Play
We are going to do a role-play. We are friends. I want to go to a new play downtown.
You want to go to a movie near where we live. Let's make a compromise.

0 1 2 3

4. Offering Suggestions/Advice
Theme: Considering Options — Episode 34

I want to learn to speak French. What can I do? Tell me at least three things.

0 1 2 3

5. Expressing Personal Opinions — Friendship
Theme: Best Friends — Episode 35

What should a best friend be like? Tell me three things.

0 1 2 3

6. Describing Things — Dream House
Theme: The Family House — Episode 35

What would your dream house be like? Tell me at least five things about it.

0 1 2 3

7. Expressing Personal Opinions — City vs. Country
Theme: City vs. Country — Episode 36

Where do you think it is better to live—the city or the country? Tell me why.

0 1 2 3

8. Expressing Humor
Theme: Humor and Jokes — Episode 36

Tell me a joke or a funny story.

0 1 2 3

ORAL EVALUATION CHECKLIST

STUDENT NAME_____

KEY: 0 = does not meet the objective   1 = meets the objective with difficulty
        2 = meets the objective adequately   3 = meets the objective with ease

OBJECTIVES

SCORE/NOTES

1. Talking about Personal Experiences — Family Holidays
Theme: Family Holiday — Episode 37

0 1 2 3

Answer this question:
What does your family do for family holidays? Describe four things.

2. Giving Advice
Themes: Giving Advice — Episode 38; Studying for Exams — Episode 39

Role-Plays
We are going to do three role-plays. I am going to tell you some problems.
You give me advice.

0 1 2 3

Part 1:
• I have a really bad cold. I have felt sick for two days.
• I need to find a new apartment. I need a place closer to school.

0 1 2 3

Part 2:
In this role-play, I am friend of yours from school. Give me at least three pieces
of advice for my problem: I am having trouble in school. My grades are not good.
I don't do well on tests. What can I do to get better grades on my exams?

3. Talking about Priorities
Theme: Managing Priorities — Episode 39

0 1 2 3

Answer these questions:
• What are some things that you have to do at home this week?
• Now tell me, which are the most important? What are you going to do first? Last?

4. Talking about Personal Experiences — Stress
Theme: Stress — Episode 39

0 1 2 3

Part 1: *Answer this question:*
• What three things give you the most stress?
• Do you think that you have a lot of stress in your life? Why or why not?

0 1 2 3

Part 2: *Answer this question:*
What do you do to relieve stress?

5. Expressing Personal Opinions — Important Things
Theme: Things That Are Important to You — Episode 40

0 1 2 3

Answer these questions:
To some people, being rich or being famous is important. What things
are important to you? Why?

6. Giving Information, Expressing Opinions — Making Money
Theme: Making Money — Episode 40

Answer these questions:
Part 1: What are some ways to make money?
Part 2: What do you think are the best ways to make money?

0 1 2 3
0 1 2 3

ORAL EVALUATION CHECKLIST

EPISODES 41-44

STUDENT NAME _____

KEY: 0 = does not meet the objective   1 = meets the objective with difficulty
        2 = meets the objective adequately   3 = meets the objective with ease

OBJECTIVES

SCORE/NOTES

1. Giving Invitations, Accepting and Refusing Invitations
Theme: Invitations — Episode 41

Role-Plays: *We are going to do two role-plays.*
Part 1: *In this role-play, I am a friend of yours. I am going to ask you out.*   0 1 2 3
*You accept the invitation. Would you like to go to the jazz concert on
Friday night? I have an extra free ticket.*
Part 2: *In this role-play, you invite me to get a coffee after class.*   0 1 2 3
You want to talk about the class assignment.
Note: Accept the invitation.

2. Expressing Personal Opinions, Talking about Personal Experiences — Waiting
Theme: Waiting — Episode 42

Answer these questions:
Part 1: *In what situations do you really hate to wait? Tell me two situations.*
Part 2: *What is the longest you ever waited for something? Tell me about it.*   0 1 2 3
                                                                        0 1 2 3

3. Expressing Personal Opinions — Education
Theme: Importance of Education — Episode 42

Why do you think it is important to learn English? Tell me two reasons.
    0 1 2 3

4. Talking about Talents and Abilities
Theme: Talent — Episode 43

Role-Play
We are going to do a role-play. You are applying for a special job. The job requires   0 1 2 3
*a person who can do many different things or who has special talents. Tell me about
the talents you have. Try to persuade me to give you the job.*
Note: Keep questioning the student to elicit information. Also, ask why the
talents are important.

5. Talking on the Phone, Taking Messages
Theme: Taking Messages — Episode 43

Role-Play
We are going to do a role-play. I am going to call you on the phone. I want to talk   0 1 2 3
*to your roommate, Jane, who is not in. You take the message. You can ask me
to repeat anything that you don't understand.*
Note: Provide students with a form like that in Episode 43, page 5.
*Hello. This is _____. Is Jane there? . . . Can I leave a message? I want her to meet me
at the café near school at 8:00 tomorrow morning so that we can study together.
She should call me at 788-2992.*
Note: Check that students fill in the key information.

6. Talking about Personal Experiences —Inspirations
Theme: Inspirations — Episode 44

Answer this question: Did a person or thing ever "inspire" you to do something?   0 1 2 3
Tell me about it.

STUDENT NAME _____

KEY: 0 = does not meet the objective   1 = meets the objective with difficulty
           2 = meets the objective adequately   3 = meets the objective with ease

OBJECTIVES

SCORE/NOTES

1. Talking about Personal Dreams and Plans
Theme: *An Ekeko — Episode 45*

Ramón gives Rebecca an ekeko. You put things that tell about your dreams on an ekeko.
Answer these questions:
- *What items would you put on your ekeko?*
- *What do they mean to you?*

0 1 2 3

2. Expressing Preferences, Expressing Opinions, Expressing Thanks — Gifts
Theme: *Exchanging Christmas Gifts — Episode 45*

Part 1: *(Show Episode 41, page 5.) You can get any gift on this page. What gift do you want? Tell me why.*

0 1 2 3

Part 2: *Now we are going to do a role-play. I have a gift for you. Here it is. Open it now.*
Note: Use any classroom prop or a picture of an item for the gift.

0 1 2 3

Part 3: *Now you are going to give gifts to family and friends. Think of three people you know. What gifts would you give to these people? Tell me why.*

0 1 2 3

3. Talking about Personal Experiences — Being Impressed
Theme: *Being Impressed — Episode 46*

To impress someone, people sometimes talk about important things they have done. What do you usually do to impress new friends?

0 1 2 3

4. Sharing Good News
Theme: *Sharing Good News — Episode 46*

Part 1: *Please respond to my statements. I have some good news.*
- *I just won a new stereo in a contest.*
- *I just got a promotion at work. I am going to have a better job.*

0 1 2 3

Part 2: Role-Play
Now we are going to do a role-play. Tell me about some good news that you have. It can be something that really happened if you want.
Note: Respond appropriately with phrases from the book.

0 1 2 3

5. Describing Someone
Theme: *A Missing Person's Report — Episode 47*

Role-Play
We are going to do a role-play. (Show students a picture of a person from a newspaper or magazine.) This person is missing. You need to describe this person to the police over the phone. I am a police officer. Tell me as much about the person as you can. Tell what the person looks like. Tell what the person is wearing.

0 1 2 3

6. Talking about Personal Habits/Preferences — New Year's Resolutions
Theme: *New Year's Resolutions — Episode 48*

Answer these questions:
- *What will your New Year's resolutions be for next year?*
- *Will you keep your resolutions? Why or why not?*

0 1 2 3

N O T E S

CLASS _____

Date	Student Name	Comments

NOTES

CLASS _____

Date	Student Name	Comments

NOTES

CLASS _____

Date	Student Name	Comments

NOTES

CLASS _____

Date	Student Name	Comments

N O T E S

Date	Student Name	Comments

N O T E S

CLASS _____

Date	Student Name	Comments

NOTES

CLASS _____

Date	Student Name	Comments